MW01279980

Making, Managing, and Milking Your Money: What Every Teen **NEEDS** to Know

By: Kristi Richards

2003

Wishing You Success!

Kristi Richards

This book is dedicated to all of the people who have inspired, supported and encouraged me throughout this endeavor. Thanks to Kathy, Paul, and Stephanie Richards, Clyde Godin, Jeffrey Jones, Kathi and Scott Cutler, and the Godin, Richards, Jones, Geroux, and Cutler families. Also thanks to my high school teachers Mrs. Bocskay and Mr. Tyler.

2003   Kristi L. Richards

TABLE OF CONTENTS

Introduction   1

  1. Chapter Introduction: Gail's Goal   3
      Chapter One: Setting Your Goals   5

* JOINING THE WORK FORCE: MAKING YOUR MONEY *

  2. Chapter Introduction: Jeff's Job Search   13
      Chapter Two: Getting a Job   15

  3. Chapter Introduction: My First Day   27
      Chapter Three: Keeping a Job and Time Management   29

  4. Chapter Introduction: Tim Gets His Tax Return   41
      Chapter Four: Filing Your Income Taxes   43

* GETTING ORGANIZED: MANAGING YOUR MONEY *

  5. Chapter Introduction: Lucy Loses Envelope   57
      Chapter Five: Creating a System   59

  6. Chapter Introduction: Sally Goes Shopping   67
      Chapter Six: The Penny Plan Budget   69

* BECOMING MONEY-WISE: MILKING YOUR MONEY *

  7. Chapter Introduction: Fred Forgets   85
      Chapter Seven: Saving Your Money   87

  8. Chapter Introduction: A Giving Experience   105
      Chapter Eight: Spending and Sharing   111

* PREPARING FOR THE FUTURE *

9.   Chapter Introduction: Samantha's Sad Day   120
      Chapter Nine: **Opening a Checking Account**   121

10.   Chapter Introduction: Credit in Your World   131
      Chapter Ten: **Obtaining Good Credit**   137

11.   Chapter Introduction: A Typical Day   143
      Chapter Eleven: **Buying a Used Car**   145

12.   Chapter Introduction: Lucy's Exciting Day   157
      Chapter Twelve: **Getting Money for College**   159

13.   Chapter Thirteen: **Reaching Your Goals**   181

Introduction

Money. Is that what this book is about? Well, not entirely. It's important to keep in my mind what money really is—paper, coins, a number on a bank statement. It in itself has little value, but what it can be exchanged for can be quite substantial. We all have things that we'd like to accomplish in life, and the truth is money is often a tool that helps us get there.

What this book is about is reaching goals, and poor money management can be as much of an obstacle as good money management can be a propeller. As a teenager, you are in a unique position to shape the direction of your life *now*. You have the chance to start off right, so that you don't have to look back and think, "I should have done this" or "If only I had done that." By reading this book, you will learn the skills that will get you where you want to go—no matter where that is.

You will learn how to apply for and keep a job, manage your time, get organized, create a budget, manage your money, learn how to save and spend wisely, buy a used car, open a checking account, obtain good credit, and get money for college. These skills will not only help you to manage your money successfully, but will also be useful in many other areas of your life, both now and in the future. Keep in mind that being rich is not the ultimate goal. Acquiring the life you desire for yourself is. Never let anything, especially money, get in the way of that.

GOALS

+ GOOD MONEY MANAGEMENT

= SUCCESS!

Gail's Goal

"Oh, come on, Mom! Marcy's mom is buying her a dress and so is Emily's."

"Well I'm not Marcy's mom, or Emily's either for that matter. You have your own job and you want *me* to pay for a dress so that you can go and have a good time at the spring dance. I pay for everything you *need.* I buy you food and clothes, but when it comes to leisure activities, you're on your own. I want you to have a good time, but I just think this is something you can manage to pay for yourself," Gail's mother stated. She was not giving in.

Gail had been trying to convince her mother to at least pay for her dress for the school's "Sponge Dance." It's called "Sponge" because the guys are supposed to sponge off of the girls, who are supposed to pay for everything. Taking tickets, pictures, and dinner into consideration, Gail wasn't sure if she could come up with the money for a new dress and accessories.

"You're the meanest mom in the whole world! Thanks a lot!" Gail screamed as she slammed her bedroom door.

"Oh, Gail I don't feel sorry for you. You know your sister will let you borrow one of her dresses, and she does have some beautiful ones so it's not as though you'll have to go looking like a bum or something. Don't be so selfish!"

Gail just had to go to the spring dance, but how could she if her mom wouldn't buy her a dress? Stay tuned for Chapter Thirteen, where you will find out how Gail will reach her goal, and how you can reach some of your goals, too.

Chapter One

Setting Your Goals

Before you can start making and saving money, you have to have a reason for doing so. You need to have a purpose for the money you earn. So write down the three things that you think you would need to be happy in life, not necessarily financial things.

1._____

2._____

3._____

Now money isn't everything. In fact, you may not even need money for the three things you listed above. Nevertheless, it may be difficult to concentrate on your goals, or even be happy, if you were totally in debt and on the verge of declaring bankruptcy. The important thing is to at least have enough money to meet your goals. For example, some of my goals are to get married, have a family, and live in a house that I own. Weddings, children, and houses all cost a lot of money. It's not the money that's important to me, it's having those things, but I need money in order to acquire them. So what are some of your goals? How will you reach the life you described in the three blanks above? Start by filling in *your* goals on the next page.

My Goals

What I want to accomplish in the next *five* years (short-term goals):

1._____

_____

2._____

_____

3._____

_____

What I want to accomplish in the next *twenty* years (longer-term goals):

1._____

_____

2._____

_____

3._____

_____

What I want to accomplish in my life (lifetime goals):

1._____

_____

2._____

_____

3._____

_____

Now pick one short-term goal that you feel is the most important to you. Make a poster stating that goal, decorate it, and post it somewhere in your room where you will see it often. This goal is going to be your main focus and every day that you see it, remember to keep working as hard as you can for it. Then, as you continue to read this book, you will develop the skills you need to make your goals more easily attainable. The final chapter will then show you how to combine all of these skills to make your goals become a reality. You'll find out how to reach goals like Gail's and many others, so stick to it and be prepared for the glorious results.

TIPS for Goal Setting

1. If you're having trouble thinking of some short-term goals, you might want to think about adding some of these to your list:

   a) Buy a used car.

   b) Go to college.

   c) Try something new.

   d) Go to *your* school dance.

   e) Get all A's on your next report card.

   f) Save a designated amount of money (example: $5000 by the time you graduate).

   g) Quit a bad habit.

   h) Start a healthier life (eat healthier or start an exercise regime).

   i) Discover one of your weaknesses and work on improving it.

   j) Get involved in an activity at school.

   k) Do something creative like write a poem or paint a picture.

   l) Start a journal.

   m) Make a scrapbook including pictures of you and all of the people who are important to you.

2. If you're having trouble thinking of some goals for the next twenty years, think about some of these:

   a) Get married.

   b) Have children.

   c) Have a career you can be proud of and happy with.

   d) Buy a house.

   e) Buy a car.

f) Take a vacation.

g) Visit a foreign country.

h) Be on track for a sound financial retirement.

3. Here are some ideas for lifetime goals: (Don't rule anything out!)

   a) Retire happily with plenty of money to enjoy life.

   b) Have tons of good stories to tell your grandkids.

   c) Save a fortune.

   d) Leave it to your family and charities when you pass away.

   e) Never stop enjoying life.

4. When setting your goals, think about those three things that you said were the most important in achieving happiness. What more specific goals can make them become a reality? By deciding what kind of life you want to lead now, you can ensure that when you're older, looking back, you'll know that you made the most of your life.

Additional Resources

Note: Check your local library for the sources listed throughout the chapters. You may even come across some other interesting books while you're at it.

<u>Books</u>

Charting Your Goals
By: Dan Dahl and Randolph Sykes
$12.95

JOINING THE WORK FORCE:

MAKING YOUR MONEY

Jeff's Job Search

Today's my big day. I'm going to apply for my first job at Zandy's Fruit Market. I have a friend that works there, and she says it's not that bad considering you're making money.

"Hi, can I please have a job application?" This is going to be pretty easy. I mean it's not like I'm applying for a *real* job.

"Sure, just fill it out and then the boss will ask you a few questions," the lady said as she handed me the application.

"Hmmm…social security number. I don't know my social security number. 'Where have I been employed recently?' I'm only fifteen. What's with all these stupid questions? All that matters is that I want the job and I'll work hard. What's the deal with all this other stuff?

"Uhh, I'm going to take this home and fill it out. I'll be back tomorrow."

"Okay," the lady said. She seemed pretty nice.

Well, I'm bummed. I wasn't prepared for any of those questions.

Chapter 2
Getting a Job

If you want to start earning, managing, and spending your *own* money, you might want to think about getting a steady job. There are many advantages to working a part-time job in high school. For one thing it can be used on future job, college, and scholarship applications. Having a job, especially for an extended amount of time, displays many good qualities about you. It shows that you are responsible, hard working, and punctual. A job also gives you the opportunity to develop important career skills and the opportunity to effectively manage your time and money. No matter how much you make at your first job, the experience you get from managing your own money will help you greatly when you start making much more.

So if you've decided you do want a steady job, you have to figure out where you want to apply. Start first by talking with your high school counselor and/or co-op director—if you have one. (Co-op is a program in which high school students can work and earn money, while also earning credit towards their diploma.) Ask friends and relatives if they know of any good positions for you, as well. If nothing turns up through these means, browse around town and ask if they're hiring at the places that interest you.

When searching for a job, look at the pay and the perks. Maybe you'd only get minimum wage at your favorite clothing store, but you also might get 15% off of anything you buy. It might be a good option for you. Also think about the skills that you will acquire in each position and how they may be helpful for the future. For example, by working in a clothing store you will develop your people skills and your ability to be a good salesperson. Finally, consider looking for a position in a company or an industry that interests you, even if it seems as though the position itself is somewhat menial. For example, if you want to be a fashion designer it may be neat to work in a clothing store, where you will always be on top of the latest styles.

Think about what you'd like to do, but remember that most jobs aren't going to be 100% fun. We all have to start somewhere, so try not to be overly picky. Now that you've thought about it, list three places that you're going to apply.

1._____

2._____

3._____

No matter what you have listed above, consider putting together a resume. It's not required, but it would make you look more professional. You've probably never made one before, but they're really quite simple. It's simply a one page summary of what type of person you are and what kind of experience you have. On the next few pages there is an example of a resume and instructions for making one. Even if you have not had formal work experience, there are still plenty of things you can include on your resume, so don't be deterred from making a resume just because of that.

Making Your Resume

Before you get started, keep in mind that your resume should, at the very least, include your name, contact information, objective, education, and work experience. You may also want to include sections for activities, hobbies, awards, skills, or references. If you do not have a lot of work experience, these may be good categories to fill the void.

1. At the top of the resume, in capital letters, type your full name (including your middle initial). Make sure it is centered.

2. Directly below your name, type your mailing address, phone number, and email address as shown on the sample resume. These should be centered also.

3. If you'd like, boldface all of the above information so that it stands out.

4. Skip a line and write "**OBJECTIVE:**" Now this is where it gets a little trickier. You need to think of what to write for your objective. The first rule is: Don't overdo it. If it sounds too embellished, it probably won't do you any good. So be honest and state why you want to work for them. Here are some general examples:

   OBJECTIVE: To begin working part-time while in school in order to broaden my skills and prepare for college.

   OBJECTIVE: To establish positive employment where I will be able to expand my capabilities.

   OBJECTIVE: To obtain a part-time position in which I will develop greater responsibility while acquiring new skills.

5. Skip a line and write "**EDUCATION:**" Write the name of your high school in bold print with the address directly beneath it. You may want to include your class level, grade point average, or any other information you feel is relevant.

6. Skip a line and write "**EXPERIENCE:**" Now if you have not had formal work experience, include your informal experience. Perhaps you have worked as a pet-sitter while your neighbors went on vacation or you mowed lawns one summer. If you ever had a paper route or

baby sat, include these items. Volunteer work can also be a valuable piece of experience.

7. Put the dates in which you worked in these occupations (estimate them if you're not sure) to the left of each position. Then provide bullet points describing your responsibilities for each one.

8. Next you can provide information on your skills, activities, hobbies, and awards. If you haven't really been involved in school or don't have a lot of awards, focus on your skills and hobbies. Think about what you like to do in your spare time and what things interest you. If you want you can include a section for "future aspirations" and discuss what you would like to do.

9. If possible, include at least one reference who is not related to you. Use a former employer, a teacher, or an adult who knows you well.

10. Remember that you can be creative with your resume. You do not need to follow the exact format shown or include all of the categories. You may also need to play around with the font size and margins in order to fit everything on one page (or fill the page as the case may be). Just make sure that it looks neat and professional.

11. Purchase some resume paper at your local office supply store and print at home, or go to a local copy center where they have resume paper available by the sheet.

Again, remember that if you don't like this style of resume, there are many more. Simply go to the library and check out a book on resume writing. You will find numerous different styles to use. There are also computer programs available that will make resume writing a breeze. Often you can use templates within your word processing software as well. See the "Additional Resources" at the end of this chapter for resources you can use to help you.

CAMERON M. LILLEY
55513 Willow
Pine Lake, MI 48256
(329) 555-1108
cml293@speedymail.com

OBJECTIVE:	To begin working part-time while in school in order to broaden my skills and prepare for college.
EDUCATION:	**Pine Lake Senior High** 25156 Maple Road Pine Lake, MI 48256 Class Level: Junior Grade point average: 3.6

EXPERIENCE:
6/00-8/00

Hope Soup Kitchen   Pine Lake, MI
Volunteer
- Served food on Saturdays.
- Assisted with cleanup.
- Delivered meals to senior citizens.

6/99-5/99

Kathryn Elliot   Pine Lake, MI
Day Care Provider
- Provided supervision for a four-year-old boy and six-year-old girl.
- Played games and did crafts with the children.
- Prepared lunch on occasion.

SKILLS:	Computer savvy, organized, good communication skills
ACTIVITIES:	Third year basketball, first year varsity Running club Students Against Drunk Driving
HOBBIES:	Fitness training, reading
AWARDS:	Honor Roll
FUTURE ASPIRATIONS:	I hope to attend the University of Michigan when I graduate and study to become a teacher.
REFERENCES:	Kathryn Elliot Samuel Franks (329) 555-1928 (329) 555-3865

Many people think that getting a minimum wage job is a cinch, but you have to apply and compete with others to get it—just like any other job. Chances are that Jeff isn't the only one applying for the job at Zandy's Fruit Market, so he's going to have to make himself stand out from the rest—in a good way. He has to fill out the application clearly and completely, look presentable, and show a little personality. Jeff wasn't prepared to fill out his job application at Zandy's Fruit Market, so on the next two pages is an example of a job application so *you* have an idea of what to expect. If you'd like, make a list of all of the information you'll need (that you know you won't remember off hand). Then take it with you to apply for the three jobs you listed previously. The layout of the job application at each place may vary, but most will ask for the same information.

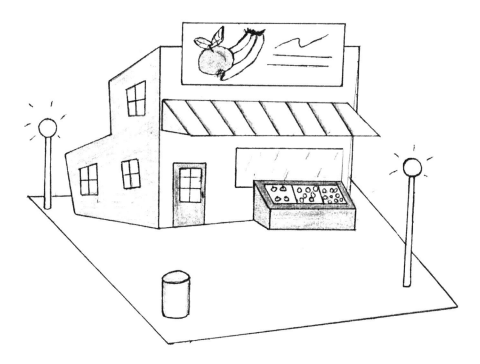

APPLICATION FOR EMPLOYMENT

PERSONAL INFORMATION

NAME (LAST NAME FIRST)	SOCIAL SECURITY NUMBER	DATE	
PRESENT ADDRESS	CITY	STATE	ZIP CODE
PERMANENT ADDRESS	CITY	STATE	ZIP CODE
PHONE NUMBER	REFERRED BY	ARE YOU 18 YEARS OR OLDER?	

EMPLOYMENT DESIRED

POSITION	DATE YOU CAN START	SALARY DESIRED	
ARE YOU EMPLOYED NOW?	IF SO, MAY WE INQUIRE OF YOUR PRESENT EMPLOYER?		
EVER APPLIED TO THIS COMPANY BEFORE?	WHERE?	WHEN?	

EDUCATION

NAME AND LOCATION	SUBJECTS STUDIED	YEARS ATTENDED	DID YOU GRADUATE?
GRAMMAR SCHOOL:			
HIGH SCHOOL:			
COLLEGE:			
TRADE, BUSINESS OR CORRESPONDENCE SCHOOL:			

GENERAL

SUBJECTS OF SPECIAL STUDY/RESEARCH WORK OR SPECIAL TRAINING/SKILLS	
U.S. MILITARY OR NAVAL SERVICE	RANK

FORMER EMPLOYERS (LIST BELOW LAST THREE EMPLOYERS, STARTING WITH LAST ONE FIRST)

DATE: MONTH AND YEAR	NAME AND ADDRESS OF EMPLOYER	SALARY	POSITION	REASON FOR LEAVING
FROM TO				
FROM TO				
FROM TO				

REFERENCES: (GIVE THE NAMES OF THREE PERSONS NOT RELATED TO YOU, WHOM YOU HAVE KNOWN FOR AT LEAST ONE YEAR)

NAME	ADDRESS	BUSINESS	YEARS KNOWN

AUTHORIZATION

"I CERTIFY THAT THE FACTS CONTAINED IN THIS APPLICATION ARE TRUE AND COMPLETE TO THE BEST OF MY KNOWLEDGE, AND I UNDERSTAND THAT IF ANY FALSE INFORMATION, OMISSIONS, OR MISREPRESENTATIONS ARE DISCOVERED, MY APPLICATION MAY BE REJECTED, AND IF I AM EMPLOYED, MY EMPLOYMENT MAY BE TERMINATED AT ANY TIME.
I AUTHORIZE INVESTIGATION OF ALL STATEMENTS CONTAINED HEREIN AND THE REFERENCES AND EMPLOYERS LISTED ABOVE TO GIVE YOU ANY AND ALL INFORMATION CONCERNING MY PREVIOUS EMPLOYMENT AND ANY PERTINENT INFORMATION THEY MAY HAVE, PERSONAL OR OTHERWISE, AND RELEASE THE COMPANY FROM ALL LIABILITY FOR ANY DAMAGE THAT MAY RESULT FROM UTILIZATION OF SUCH INFORMATION."

DATE   SIGNATURE

Final TIPS for Getting the Job

1) **Be clean and neat when you go in.** Wear appropriate clothes for the job interview. If it's a business-like atmosphere, dress up a bit. If it's a fast food restaurant, don't overdo it. Wear something clean and simple.

2) **Be courteous and polite.**

3) **Be honest.** Don't lie to try to make it look like you have more experience than you do. If you lie and you do get the job, it may soon become obvious that you didn't have the experience you claimed to.

4) **Be yourself.** Let them see what kind of person you are and why they should hire you.

5) **Show them that you're willing to work.**

6) **Make sure that your application is filled out neatly and completely.** Triple check for spelling errors, both in your application and in your resume. Then have a teacher or parent review them. A spelling error or sloppy application can be a big turn-off for your prospective employers.

Mainly, employers want to hire people who are hard working, punctual, easy going, and honest. If you are those things, simply show that you are, and you'll probably have a pretty good shot. So get out there and do the best you can. If you don't get one of your first three choices, simply pick three more and try again. Think about what might have prevented you from getting hired and try to revise your plan for next time. Soon something will come up.

Additional Resources

Books for Resume Writing

Resumes for the First-Time Job Hunter
$9.95

Resume Writing Made Easy
By: Lola M. Coxford
$11.95

Resumes: for People Who Hate to Write Resumes
By: Jack W. Wright
$12.95

The Complete Idiot's Guide to the Perfect Resume
$16.95

Other Resume Writing Tools

A Job Winning Resume with Your Computer
(Instructive video and computer disk)
Check your library.

Books on Getting the Job and Interviewing

What You Need to Know About Getting a Job and Filling Out Forms
By: Carolyn Morton Starkey and Norgina Wright Penn

Your First Interview
By: Ron Fry
$9.95

Websites

http://www.jobweb.com/Resumes_Interviews/resume_guide/restips.html

http://www.myfuture.com

My First Day

"I'm so confused. What do I do? Look at all of those people. They're all going to scream at me if they don't get their food fast." Those were my thoughts on my first day of working at the restaurant.

"Shawn, give Kristi a hand up there. She's lost."

Shawn showed me what to do, but still I felt overwhelmed. I felt that way probably for the first month. Every Saturday, the only time I worked when it was really busy, I would mess something up. I almost even quit. Why should I work when my friends were all lazy bums mooching off of their parents? The truth is I didn't want to mooch. I wanted to make *my own* money and do whatever I wanted with it. So quitting wasn't what I really wanted, but I didn't know what else to do because it seemed like I wasn't getting anywhere. My family convinced me to try it for one more day. I tried so hard, and because I thought I was going to quit anyway, I didn't have so much pressure on me. I did everything as fast and perfect as I could. It was then that I realized I could do it after all. From that day on, I was more confident, and I began to do a really good job.

Many people do not think that working in a restaurant, or any other teenage job, is difficult, but when you've never done it before, you don't know where anything is, what the system is, or where the buttons on the cash register are--it's not so easy. It takes practice--for *anybody*. You may feel the same way as I did when you start your new job, but give yourself time to get used to everything and pretty soon things will fall into place.

Chapter Three
Keeping a Job and Time Management

Now that you have a job, you should try to keep it. First rule: Always give a job at least a one-month trial period. Don't quit after the first week, even if you really hate it. The first week is almost always rough, especially if it's your first job, so expect it. I hated my first job and I wanted to quit, but my mom gave me the advice I just gave you, and then I worked there all through high school. I'm glad I stayed. The second thing is to accept the fact that the job probably isn't exactly glamorous. You might have to do a lot of cleaning and dealing with the public. It depends on what kind of job you get. I worked at a restaurant where I washed dishes, swept, mopped, rang up customers, and filled orders, but I also worked with nice people and got free food. Altogether it wasn't so bad. Also, since I worked there for a long time, I got paid more than most of my friends who had hopped from job to job. Don't forget that the longer you work somewhere, the more you get paid. It also shows dedication when you apply for a job in the future and when you apply to college.

One major change is going to occur when you get a job, so be prepared. You're not going to have as much free time as you did in the past. Even working fifteen hours a week is going to require some planning. You have to remember that school is important now so you probably don't want to work much more than fifteen hours a week. You want to have time to get your homework done and have some time to hang out a little bit. So, your money is not the only thing you want to stretch. You want to try and stretch your time to the limit, too. First thing's first, we have to make a schedule. On the next page, write down the things that you must do and would like to do in order of importance. Next to each priority, write the number of hours required for that activity each week. You can use the example provided as a guide.

Things I Must Do (First Priorities):

_____

_____

_____

_____

_____

_____

_____

_____

_____

_____

Things I Want to Do (Second Priorities):

_____

_____

_____

_____

_____

_____

_____

_____

_____

_____

_____

Total number of hours in a week: (24 x 7 = 168)   168

1. **Total number of hours for things you *must* do each week:**

   (add up all of the hours in the 1st priority group)   _____

2. **Total number of hours for things you *want* to do each week:**

   (add up all of the hours in the 2nd priority group)   _____

3. **Total hours for things you must and want to do each week:**

   (add Line 1 and Line 2)   _____

4. **Total number of hours remaining:**

   (Subtract Line 3 from 168)   _____

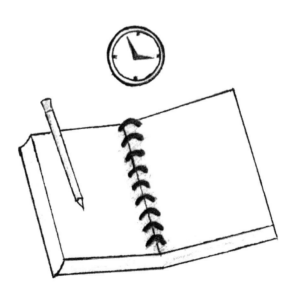

(Example:)

List of Things That I Must Do and Want to Do Weekly

Things I Must Do (First Priorities):

1. sleep (8 hours a night, 56 hours a week)

2. eat dinner (1 hour a day, 7 hours a week)

3. go to school (including breakfast, lunch, the amount of time it takes to
   get up, get ready, drive to school, go to my classes and get home:
   8 hours a day, 40 hours a week)

4. do homework (15 hours)

Things I Want to Do (Second Priorities):

1. go to work (14 hours)

2. go to church (2 hours)

3. go to school activities (1 hours)

4. join running club (4 hours)

Total number of hours in a week: 168hours

1. **Total number of hours for things I must do each week:**   118hours

2. **Total number of hours for things I want to do each week:**   21 hours

3. **Total number of hours for things I must and want to do:**   139 hours

4. **Total number of hours remaining:**   29 hours

Now the question is: Are there enough hours in the week to do everything that you must and want to do? Do you have enough remaining hours for yourself? You do not want every hour spoken for. You should at least have 25 free hours where you do not have set obligations. If you do not, you should probably make some adjustments. Since you have listed everything in order of importance, start from the bottom of the "want to do" column and try to cut out any hours you can. For example, you might want to cut back on the number of activities you're involved in. Try not to cut back too much on the things that are the most important to you or that you really enjoy. If you have a job and feel overwhelmed because you are having difficulty meeting your other priorities, such as doing well in school or getting enough sleep, then you should consider cutting your work hours. If you don't have 25 free hours, but you really don't want to cut anything out and you don't feel overwhelmed, then leave things as they are. You may be the type of person who likes a hectic lifestyle and there is no reason for you to compromise or sell yourself short on the things you like to do.

Now that you know what your responsibilities are and you know how much time you have each week to complete them, it would be helpful to create a specific schedule. Honestly, you're not going to follow your schedule to exactness, but you'll get an idea for when to do what and will probably get into the habit of following that schedule unconsciously. On the next two pages is an example of a schedule. On a separate sheet of paper follow the example and make up your own schedule.

Weekly Schedule

SUNDAY

9:00 a.m.-9:50 a.m.	Get up. Get ready for church.
9:50 a.m.-11:10 a.m.	Go to church.
11:10 a.m.-3:00 p.m.	Do homework.
3:00 p.m.-5:00 p.m.	MY TIME!
5:00 p.m.-6:00 p.m.	Eat dinner.
6:00 p.m.-10:00 p.m.	MY TIME!
10:00 p.m.	Go to sleep.

MONDAY

6:30 a.m.-7:15 a.m.	Get up. Get ready for school.
7:15 a.m.-3:00 p.m.	Go to school.
3:00 p.m.-5:00 p.m.	Running Club
5:00 p.m.-6:00 p.m.	Eat dinner.
6:00 p.m.-9:00 p.m.	Do homework.
9:00 p.m.-10:00 p.m.	MY TIME!
10:00 p.m.	Go to sleep.

TUESDAY

6:30 a.m.-7:15 a.m.	Get up. Get ready for school.
7:15 a.m.-3:00 p.m.	Go to school.
3:00 p.m.-6:30 p.m.	Go to work.
6:30 p.m.-8:30 p.m.	Do homework.
8:30 p.m.-10:00 p.m.	MY TIME!
10:00 p.m.	Go to sleep.

WEDNESDAY

6:30 a.m.-7:15 a.m.	Get up. Get ready for school.
7:15 a.m.-3:00 p.m.	Go to school.
3:00 p.m.-3:30 p.m.	Club meeting.
3:30 p.m.-5:00 p.m.	Do homework.
5:00 p.m.-6:00 p.m.	Eat dinner.
6:00 p.m.-7:30 p.m.	Do homework.
7:30 p.m.-10:00 p.m.	MY TIME!
10:00 p.m.	Go to sleep.

THURSDAY

6:30 a.m.-7:15 a.m.	Get up. Get ready for school.
7:15 a.m.-3:00 p.m.	Go to school.
3:00 p.m.-5:00 p.m.	Running Club
5:00 p.m.-6:00 p.m.	Eat Dinner.
6:00 p.m.-9:00 p.m.	Do homework.
9:00 p.m.-10:00 p.m.	MY TIME!
10:00 p.m.	Go to sleep.

FRIDAY

6:00 a.m.-7:00 a.m.	Get up. Get ready for school.
7:00 a.m.-7:30 a.m.	Club meeting.
7:30 a.m.-3:00 p.m.	Go to school.
3:00 p.m.-6:30 p.m.	Go to work.
6:30 p.m.-12:00 a.m.	MY TIME!
12:00 a.m.	Go to sleep.

SATURDAY

8:00 a.m.-9:00 a.m.	Get up. Get ready for work.
9:00 a.m.-3:30 p.m.	Go to work.
3:30 p.m.-5:00 p.m.	MY TIME!
5:00 p.m.-6:00 p.m.	Eat dinner.
6:00 p.m.-12:00 a.m.	MY TIME!
12:00 a.m.	Go to sleep.

According to this schedule, I would spend the following amounts of time in each category. (Total: 168 hours)

School:	42.5	hours
Work:	13.5	hours
Sleep:	59	hours
Church:	1.5	hours
Activities:	1	hour
Running Club:	4	hours
Homework:	15	hours
MY TIME!:	25	hours
Eating:	5	hours
Other:	1.5	hours

These figures come out very close to the ones I predicted. This is good because you want your schedule to reflect the amount of time you're going to spend in each category. Another thing you might have noticed is that the schedule was very similar for each day during the week. The pattern was to get up, go to school, participate in school activities or work, come home, do some homework, then relax a little bit. (The weekend was a little bit different because I wanted to take a short break from homework and allow myself more free time.) Anyway, the <u>pattern</u> that your schedule forms is what you're looking for. You don't need to follow the schedule exactly, but following the general pattern can help you out.

Another good way to manage your time well is to start each day by doing the things you want to do **least**. That way when you finish all of the stuff you didn't want to do, like homework for example, then everything else is downhill. If you do the things you want to first, then you may get caught up in having so much fun that you find yourself neglecting your more important priorities or you won't have as good of a time because all the while you'll be dreading doing your chores or homework later. It's best to come home and do your homework, as well as any other chores or unattractive activities you have to do, right away. Then, when you go out, you don't have to worry about it anymore.

Managing your time well is a very important aspect of not only keeping a job, but also in doing well in school and fulfilling your other priorities. Once you get time management down, there are some other simple things that you can do in the work place itself to increase your chances of keeping your job and even getting a raise.

TIPS for Keeping Your Job

1) **Do your best!**

2) **Don't just be on time—BE EARLY!!!**

3) **Never miss work unless you have to, and always give as much notice as possible.**

4) **Don't complain.**

5) **Be kind, courteous, and polite, especially to the customers if you interact with them.**

6) **If you don't know something—ask.** You're always going to be better off to simply ask, then to guess and do it wrong.

7) **Be neat and clean when you go to work and wear the proper attire, whatever it may be.** Some places will want you to wear the company T-shirt. Other places will require you to dress up.

8) **Work hard, even if the boss isn't looking.** You're being paid to work.

9) **Be helpful and kind to your co-workers.** If you're going to work together, it's best that you get along.

10) **Be confident in yourself, and stay committed to your responsibilities.**

Additional Resources

<u>Books</u>

Managing Your Time
By: Ron Fry
$4.95

The Ten Natural Laws of Successful Time and Life Management
By: Hyrum W. Smith
$21.45

Tim Gets His Tax Return

"It's here! It's here!"

"What are you so excited about Tim?" his mother inquired.

"I got my tax refund back. Two-hundred dollars!"

"That's great. What are you planning on doing with that money?"

"I've decided that I'm going to buy myself a new pair of inline skates for the summer."

"Are you expecting any money back from the state?"

"Yeah, I should get $60 back from them," Tim answered.

"Good. Then you can buy yourself a helmet, knee pads, elbow pads, wrist guards, and ... some other good safety stuff."

Getting your tax return can be kind of exciting. It's your own money that you'll be getting back, but it feels kind of like a free gift. If you've been working, you'll have to file your income taxes, and there's no guarantee that you'll get a refund. However, because the first four thousand dollars or more (the amount changes from year to year) that you make *is not taxed by the federal government*, you can usually expect a refund. Read the next chapter to figure out how much you can expect and then start thinking about what *you'd* like to do with it.

Chapter Four

Filing Your Income Taxes

You might have heard the phrase, "there are only two things you *must* do—die and pay taxes." Well, it's true. Everyone has to pay taxes, and if you have a job you've gotta do it, too. Your taxes will be taken directly out of your check every week, and you should get a "check stub" showing your hourly wage, how many hours you worked that period, your gross wages (how much you made before any taxes were taken out), how much was taken out for various taxes, your annualized wages and taxes paid, and finally how much money is left over for you. Below is an example of a check stub, but they will take many different styles and forms.

EARNINGS STATEMENT

		CHECK NO.	001419
		CHECK DATE	9/12/01
		PERIOD ENDING	9/07/01

NAME
TIMOTHY STERLING

2001-0022
MELINDA'S COPYING AND OFFICE SUPPLY
28367 Cedar
Daveno, MI 53465

EMPLOYEE NO	SOCIAL SECURITY NO.	DEPT	MAR STAT	FED EXP	STATE EXP	LOC EXP	TAX FREQ
2	444-29-5255	100	S	00	00		WK

PAY TYPE	RATE	HOURS (UNITS)	CURRENT EARNINGS	YEAR-TO-DATE EARNINGS	TAXES AND DEDUCTIONS	CURRENT	YEAR-TO-DATE	OTHER INFORMATION
REGULAR	8.250	12.50	103.13	8050.85	FICA	7.89	631.93	
OVERTIME				210.38	FIT	7.81	919.87	
					MI	4.54	363.52	

TOTAL HOURS ➤ 12.50	TOTAL EARNINGS		TOTAL TAXES & DEDUCTIONS	NET CHECK
CURRENT ➤	103.13		20.24	82.89
YEAR-TO-DATE ➤	8261.23		1915.32	

MEMORANDUM	DIRECT DEPOSIT DISTRIBUTIONS
TAX TIME IS QUICKLY APPROACHING!! PLEASE VERIFY YOUR SOCIAL SECURITY #, NAME, ADDRESS, AND TAX INFORMATION.	

Understanding Your Check Stub

1) Of course your check stub will include some basic information like your name, social security number, your place of employment and address, the date of the check, and the date of the period end for the check. The period end is the last day of your payment cycle. So if your pay period runs from Monday through Friday for two weeks and then you get paid the following Friday, your period ending date will be one week prior to the check date. In the example, the pay period is one week long running from Thursday to Wednesday with payment on Monday.

2) Your check stub should also include information about your marital status and tax withholding selections. In the example there is an "S" in the "MAR STAT" column, which indicates that the employee is single. The next two columns, "FED. EXP." and "STATE EXP.," indicate federal and state exemptions. What this indicates is how many people are dependent on you for support. Since you are probably claimed as a dependent on your parents' taxes, and presumably are not married with children, you should have zero's in these columns. (All this means is that your parents take care of you.)

3) The frequency of your pay period is indicated under "TAX FREQ." In the example it shows "WK," which indicates that this individual is paid weekly.

4) Now for "PAY TYPE" it shows "REGULAR" in the example, which means that these were ordinary work hours at the person's regular wage rate. If a person were to work over forty hours it would indicate the number of "OVERTIME" hours, as well. Overtime hours would be paid at the rate of one-and-a-half times the person's regular rate. So if you get paid $7/hour and you worked over forty hours you would

get paid $10.50/hour for every hour over forty. However, since you are a teenager, this should hopefully not occur very often, and if you are under the age of sixteen it is actually illegal to work more than forty hours. (Note that not all employees receive overtime pay for hours worked beyond the standard forty hour week. Often salaried professionals do not.) Another type of payment could occur if you work on a holiday, in which time-and-a-half or double-pay may apply. The "RATE" will indicate how much you were paid for each set of hours worked.

5) "HOURS (UNITS)" shows how many hours you worked during the pay period.

6) "CURRENT EARNINGS" shows your earnings before taxes, which is equal to the number of hours worked times the pay rate. If different pay rates apply it is the sum of each product.

7) "YEAR-TO-DATE EARNINGS" shows how much you have earned since January 1st of that year, before taxes have been subtracted.

8) In the example, "TAXES AND DEDUCTIONS" include FICA, FIT, and MI. FICA stands for Federal Insurance Contributions Act and includes the money that is automatically deducted for Social Security and Medicare. FIT shows the money taken out for Federal Income Taxes and MI shows the state income taxes withheld. It is MI in this example because it is for the state of Michigan. You can see the taxes withheld in each category for the current check and for the year so far.

9) "TOTAL TAXES & DEDUCTIONS" show the total amount of money that was withheld from this check and how much has been withheld for the entire year.

10) Finally, the "NET CHECK" amount will be shown, which is how much you actually get to keep.

Note: Keep in mind that what you actually pay in federal and state taxes will be adjusted at the end of the year, in which case you may receive money back or owe money. However, FICA dollars are always taken out of your check in the exact amount you owe. You will never receive a refund for paying too much in FICA taxes, nor will you ever owe more. Currently, about 7.65% of your check goes toward FICA taxes. However, this amount may change as tax laws are amended.

NOTE: This chapter, as is the rest of the book, is intended to be used as a guide. It is not meant to serve as tax counsel. Please consult a C.P.A. or other tax professional to assess your situation.

Understanding Taxes

The reason why taxes can be so complicated is that not everyone has to pay the same amount. Everyone is exempt from paying taxes on a minimum amount of money, but depending on how many children a person has, etc. many people have additional deductions. An **exemption**, or **deduction**, is money that can be subtracted from your taxable wages, which means a person doesn't have to pay taxes on that amount. For example, let's say a divorced woman with two children makes $35,000 a year. Because she has three people to take care of (including herself) she has more financial obligations than a single woman with no children. The government will then exempt her from paying taxes on a specified amount of money for each person that depends on her financially. In other words, she does not have to pay taxes on *all* of the money she made. After the exemptions, she may only need to pay taxes on $22,000. A single person making $35,000, however, does not have as many financial obligations, and thus will have to pay taxes on a higher percentage of her wages. She may need to pay taxes on $28,000. This is done to recognize that some people have more challenging financial situations, so they are slightly compensated for by not having to pay taxes on as much of their earnings.

At the end of each year, some people have paid more taxes than what they owe and others have not paid enough, which is why taxes are filed. People who have paid too much have to figure out exactly how much they deserve back, and people who have paid too little have to figure out exactly how much they owe. Fortunately for you, most teenagers fall into the category of people who get money back from the government at the year's end, but getting a large refund when you're making a sizable income may not be a good idea.

Once you get older you don't want to overpay the government by a large amount just so you can get a refund at the end of the year because it's like giving the government a free loan. They're holding your money until the end of the year for their use, while you're losing interest that could have been gained on it. When you're only making a small amount, this is not a big issue because the interest would be minute, but beware when you begin making a larger salary.

***Tip: Although this is sound advice for most, if you are the type who has a very hard time saving and find overpaying the government to be a good savings mechanism, it may not be a bad idea. If you wouldn't have saved the money anyway, you didn't lose any interest, so you could be better off. It just depends on your personality type—whether you'd rather have the money at *your* disposal for savings and investment throughout the year or you'd rather let the government be your piggy bank. ***

Each person's tax records cover an entire calendar year, from January 1 to December 31. By law, your employer and/or any other place that you have earned money (ex. a bank or credit union) must send you a tax document by January 31. The tax document from your employer is called a W-2 form.

You should always keep your last check stub to compare with your W-2 for possible errors. Below is an example of a W-2 form.

a Control number 529717-00003	115963 020076	This information is being furnished to the Internal Revenue Service. If You are required to file a tax return, a negligence penalty or other sanction may be imposed on you if this income is taxable and you fail to report it.		
b Employer's identification number 11-5560909		1 Wages, tips, other compensation 9509.06	2 Federal income tax withheld 1038.17	EMPLOYEE'S COPY
c Employer's name, address, and ZIP code MELINDA'S COPYING AND OFFICE SUPPLY 28367 CEDAR DAVENO, MI 53465		3 Social security wages 9509.06	4 Social security tax withheld 589.50	
		5 Medicare wages and tips 9509.06	6 Medicare tax withheld 137.88	
		7 Social security tips	8 Allocated tips	
d Employee's social security number 444-29-5255		9 Advance EIC payment	10 Dependent care benefits	KEEP THE TOP PORTION OF THIS FORM FOR YOUR RECORDS.
e Employee's name, address, and ZIP code 0000 TIMOTHY STERLING 1522 GLENDALE DAVENO MI 53465		11 Nonqualified plans	12 Benefits included in Box 1	
		13 See Instr. for Form W-2	14 Other	THE SUBSTITUTE W2 FORMS PROVIDED BELOW SHOULD BE FILED WITH YOUR FEDERAL, STATE AND LOCAL TAX RETURNS
		15 Statutory Deceased Pension employee plan	Legal 942 Subtotal Deferred rep. emp. compensation	
16 State Employer's state I.D. No. MI ME-1214351	17 State wages, tips, etc. 9509.06	18 State income tax 418.42	19 Locality name 20 Local wages, tips, etc. 21 Local income tax	

Department of the Treasury--Internal Revenue Service

Form **W-2** Wage and Tax Statement **2002**
Copy C For EMPLOYEE'S RECORDS (See Notice on back.)

For Paperwork Reduction Act Notice, see separate instructions.
OMB No. 1545-0008

DETACH AND FILE WITH FEDERAL RETURN   DETACH AND FILE WITH STATE RETURN   DETACH AND FILE WITH LOCAL RETURN

A person has until April 15 to complete his or her tax form and get it to the post office. If you're expecting a refund, you'll probably want to mail it much sooner, because then you will receive your refund sooner.

The tax form you will most likely be using is called the 1040EZ. It is the easiest to use. You can pick up a copy at the library, post office, or call the IRS at 1-800-829-3676 (1-800-TAX-FORM). Even easier—you can download it from the internet at http://www.irs.gov/forms_pubs/forms.html. Once you've filed, the IRS has you on record and will mail you your forms automatically the following year.

Your Situation:

Typically, most teenagers are claimed as dependents on their parents' form, which means that their parents claim responsibility for taking care of them to get a tax deduction for that extra expense.

Filling Out the Form

Although the form may change from year to year, you will often have to provide the same information.

Note: Write everything in pencil initially because you may make some mistakes. After you have completed the form and checked for errors, write over the pencil with black ink, or print a new form and rewrite the information in black ink.

A) Personal Information

1. -If this is your first time filing you won't have an IRS label, so in the box that says "Use the IRS label here," you are simply going to fill in your first name, middle initial, last name, address, and your spouse's name if you are married. If you are not married, leave the space provided for spouse's name blank.

   -If you have an IRS label, stick it on here.

2. Fill in your social security number in the boxes provided to the right of your name and address. Again if you are not married leave the spaces for "Spouse's social security number" blank.

3. If you want to have $3 (or the amount shown) of your tax money to go to the Presidential Election Campaign, check the "Yes" box. If not, check "No." Either way your tax refund will not be affected.

B) Tax Information

-Income-

1. One of the first things you will be required to report is the amount of your total gross wages. This should be shown in box one of your W-2. If you worked at more than one place and have more than one W-2, add together all of the money you have earned and write that amount here.

2. Next, you will need to report the amount of money you have earned from interest on a bank account or from other investments. Currently, if the interest you earned is over $400, you cannot use this form.

3. It will also ask if you've had unemployment compensation. (You would enter a value if you were unemployed at some point during the year and you received money from the government in the form of unemployment compensation.)

4. Your total gross wages, interest income, and unemployment compensation added together equal your total gross income.

5. –The form will also ask if someone else claims you as a dependent. Most likely your parent(s) and/or guardian(s) claim you on their form, so you would say "Yes."

    -If you are not claimed as a dependent on someone else's form, then you should say "No."

6. Based on your marital status and whether or not someone claims you as a dependent, you will have a designated standard deduction. This means that out of all the money you made, you don't have to pay taxes on a certain amount of it. For example, if you made $12,000 and the deduction in your case was $5,000 you would only have to pay taxes on $7,000. In other words, your total income minus your deduction equals your **taxable income**. Note that if you made less than the standard deduction your answer will be negative so you are not responsible for paying any federal taxes. (This means that all of the money that you have already paid in federal taxes will be returned to you.)

-Payments and tax

7. The form will require you to indicate the total amount of federal taxes withheld from your checks throughout the year. This amount is shown in box 2 of your W-2 form. The total amount of taxes you have paid to the government throughout the year is called your **total payments**.

8. Once you know your taxable income, which you determined in step 6, you can determine how much you owe. The form gives the pages in the tax booklet in which you can find this amount.

9. If the amount of taxes you paid is more than the amount of taxes you owe, you get a refund. The amount you will get back is equal to the difference between the two (taxes paid minus taxes owed). If you're getting a refund, you can have it sent directly to your bank. Just fill out the routing number, the type of account, and your account number.

10. If the amount you paid is less than what you owe, you will have to enclose a payment for the difference. Since you should never send cash through the mail, you may need your parents to write you a check and you can give them the money in cash. If that is not possible, you can go to your local drugstore and obtain a money order.

11. At the end of the tax form you will need to sign your name, date it, and write your occupation.

12. Finally, if you received your form in the mail, use the pre-addressed envelope provided to mail the completed form in. Otherwise use the address shown in your tax booklet.

You're Done!!!

TIPS for Filing Your Income Taxes

1) **Fill out the form neatly and completely.**

2) **Make sure you've filled in everything necessary.** Go down the list, and for every line number make sure you have filled in the appropriate information.

3) **Check your math.** Repeat the calculations at least twice to make sure that you didn't make a calculator error or forget something.

4) **Don't forget your signature at the bottom.**

5) **File as early as possible if you are expecting a return.** The sooner you mail it, the sooner you'll get your refund. If you wait until April 15, you may not receive your refund until June.

6) **Take your time.** Don't rush through it. The form is very simple and probably won't take you very long anyway.

7) **Have a parent double check the form for errors.**

8) **Make copies of the forms and keep the tax records for at least seven years.** The IRS reserves the right to dispute the information you provide in your tax forms and you may need to show proof of what you stated. It's also a good idea to keep them so that you can compare your wages and taxes each year. I never dispose of my tax information, no matter how long it's been.

9) The instructions given in this chapter are for your *federal* taxes, not your state taxes. Each state will do things differently, so **review the instructions carefully before beginning your *state* tax forms.** However, once you've completed your federal forms, the state forms should be fairly simple.

10) Another option is to file your taxes online via the internet. E-filing is expected to be the predominate means of filing by the end of this decade.

Additional Resources

Phone Numbers

1-800-829-1040	IRS tax help line
1-800-TAX-FORM	Request tax forms via this number

Guides

Ernst & Young's Tax Guide   Official tax guide of the IRS

Websites

http://www.irs.gov   Official IRS website

GETTING ORGANIZED:

MANAGING YOUR MONEY

Lucy Loses Envelope

"Mom! What did you do with that envelope I set on the TV?"

"What envelope?"

"I specifically remember leaving it on the television yesterday. Where did you put it?"

"Where did *I* put it? What envelope are you talking about?"

"It has my scholarship application for the university in it, and it's due in two days, I've got to get it to the post office *today*!" Lucy was hysterical. She had just gotten her scholarship application prepared yesterday and she was going to mail it today, but now she can't find it anywhere.

"Why are you always moving things around anyway? Now what am I going to do? I could fill out another application, but I can't get any copies of the recommendations until tomorrow. I don't know if it will get there in time if I don't mail it today."

Despite Lucy's rudeness, her mother was sympathetic and together they began to search the house. Lucy's mom was hoping that she hadn't misplaced it—she did have a tendency to move things around.

"Aha! Here it is. Right here in *your* book bag. I don't think you can blame me anymore," her mother was relieved. "Well, you better get to the post office."

"Sorry, mom. I was just so sure I had left it on the TV"

Sometimes it's easy to misplace things. It's just fortunate that Lucy's application was found. In order to prevent this type of thing from happening to you, read on and learn how to organize everything that's important to you.

Chapter Five
Creating a System

Now that you've set your goals, gotten a job, and organized your schedule, it's time to create a system for organizing your finances. Most of the time, it works best to have a filing system with separate folders labeled for your *own* needs. Below is a list of "must have" folders.

Finance

F1.   Budget

F2.   Bills to be Paid

F3.   Expenditures

F4.   Income Records

F5.   Receipts

     a) Bank Receipts

     b) Clothing Receipts

     c) Gift Receipts

     d) Other Receipts

F6.   Savings Account-Bank Statements

F7.   Tax Records

F8.   Warranties

Personal

P1.   Automobile

P2.   Career

P3.   Goals

P4.   Job Search

P5.   Leisure

P6.   Resume

P7.   Schedule

In your finance section, you're going to have any folders that deal with money. Following is a brief description of what you can put in each folder.

F1. Budget - In the next chapter we're going to create a budget. You can keep a copy in this folder.

F2. Bills to be Paid - In this folder you can keep IOUs to your friends or relatives, bills for magazine subscriptions, and/or a list of how much, if anything, you have to pay for car insurance, etc. I keep a chart like the one shown on page 62 in my "Bills to be Paid" file, which lists how much money I owe my Mom each month for car insurance, and I mark the date in each box after I pay it.

F3. Expenditures - This is where you're going to keep a running list of your expenditures using a system I'll explain in the next chapter.

F4. Income Records - This is where you should keep all of your check stubs from work.

F5. Receipts - This is where should store all of your receipts. For example, you should always keep receipts for clothing (in case you find out that there's a hole in your new shirt), any gifts that you buy (in case they don't like it or something is wrong with it), and receipts from the bank for any deposits or withdrawals. It's a good idea to compare your information with the bank's. I've never caught any errors, but it's good to double check. (If you don't have a bank account yet, stay tuned for Chapter Seven.) You should also have another section for miscellaneous receipts.

***Note: Over time these receipts may build up, so every month or two go through and clean out the ones you can dispose of. ***

F6. Savings Account-Bank Statements - This is a storage place for the bank statements you receive in the mail. These are the statements you can use to double check the bank's information with *your* bank receipts.

F7. Tax Records - This is for copies of your tax forms and other related information. Remember, you should keep a copy of all your records for at least seven years.

F8. Warranties - This is where you should keep all of your warranties. As soon as you buy something that comes with a warranty, such as a stereo or television, staple the receipt to the warranty and put it in your file. If anything goes wrong with the product later on, you won't have to turn the house upside down looking for your warranty and receipt. You should occasionally review your warranties and discard the ones that have expired.

Car Insurance Payments 2003		
Month	Amount	Date Paid
January	$85	1/15/2003
February	$85	2/13/2003
March	$85	3/13/2003
April	$85	4/15/2003
May	$85	5/16/2003
June	$0	X
July	$85	
August	$85	
September	$85	
October	$85	
November	$85	
December	$85	

Under the **Personal** category, you're going to keep any files you want for things that are personal to you.

P1. Automobile - If you don't have a car yet, it's still a good idea to create an "Automobile" folder. We'll talk about buying a used car in Chapter Eleven, but in the meantime keep clippings of cars you like from the newspaper or from research you have done on the internet. If you do have a car, use this folder to keep track of oil changes, repairs, or general maintenance performed. If you ever decide to sell the car, you should always be able to provide this information to the new owner. It is also useful to keep track of when it's time to get new tires, your next tune-up, or your next oil change.

P2. Career - This is where you should keep plans for your future occupation. For example, if you went to a seminar at school that focused on a particular career of interest, chances are good that you received a couple of pamphlets regarding that career. This would be the type of thing that you would put in your career file. You can include information about the college(s) you want to attend or create a separate folder for that.

P3. Goals - We talked about goals in Chapter One. As you continually make new goals, short-term and long-term, you can place them in this folder.

P4. Job Search - This folder involves your current job search, whereas the file folder titled "Career" is used for planning for a future career. You can put the names and addresses of the companies you said you might like to work at in Chapter Two. If you want, you can also put the copy of the job application you filled out in Chapter Two in this folder.

P5. Leisure - The folder labeled "Leisure" is especially for you and what you like to do for fun. You can put clippings for a show you want to see or an amusement park you want to go to, or if you're planning on going somewhere for Spring Break, you can put your travel plans in this folder.

P6. Resume - We made a resume in Chapter Two, and you should keep a copy of it in this folder.

P7. Schedule - You can use this folder to put a copy of the schedule you made in Chapter Three.

Now that you have the basic folders, you should be fully equipped to keep track of all the necessary things. Remember, you may need additional folders for your own individual purposes, so feel free to add some anytime.

The reason why it's good to have a system of folders is because it keeps everything organized. As you grow older, good organization will become more important. You'll have to know what bills are due when and how much money you have available to pay them. The more organized you become now, the more prepared you will be in the future. Plus, it's a good idea to keep all of your important things in one place so that nothing gets lost. Now if you don't like the filing system, you can always try a different system—as long as you have one. You may want to use a combination of things. For example, a cash box for receipts and warranties, and a couple of binders with separate sections for bank statements, expenditures, and personal materials. The filing method usually works best, but if you like something else better, go for it! Whatever you are most comfortable with will be the most beneficial to you.

TIPS for You and Your System

1) **Be organized.** Whatever your system is, know where everything is at and have some form of division between separate items.

2) **Don't be afraid to add new folders when necessary.** Around your junior or senior year, you might want to create a folder for financial aid opportunities for further education. A matter like this requires organization so that you don't miss the deadlines. Whatever the purpose, if there's not already a folder for it--create one.

3) **Jazz up your folders if you want.** Maybe you don't want an average manila folder, so draw a picture on it or color some designs. Add your own creative touch.

4) **Put the folders in an order that makes sense to you.** I put them in alphabetical order, but you could put them in order of subject or importance. Organize them any way you want, but make sure it's a way that you can find something fast.

Additional Resources

Books

Go For It: Get Organized
By: Sara Gilbert
$6.95

Sally Goes Shopping

"Wow! One hundred dollars! Baby-sitting really pays off sometimes."

Sally was really excited. She had started her first regular baby-sitting job this summer. She watches two children, for twenty hours a week, while their mother is at work.

"Hi, Mary. You wanna come to the mall with me? I just got my first payment for baby-sitting."

"Sure, Sally. I'll be right over."

The two girls shopped all day. Sally even treated her friend Mary to lunch and an ice cream cone. She also bought two new shirts and a new pair of jeans.

"This is so much fun! Let's go see a movie." Sally felt as though she were rich. She never had so much money to spend all at once.

"Yeah, good idea," Mary agreed.

After the long day came to an end, Sally plopped down and looked in her wallet to see how much money she had left.

"My money! I lost my money! I must have dropped it somewhere. I only have $8 left." Sally was rummaging through her pockets to see if she could find any spare dollars she might have shoved in there.

"Well, Sally, those jeans were $30, the two shirts were $35, lunch was $15, and you spent about $12 at the movies by the time you bought snacks. That adds up to . . . about $92. I don't think you lost any money Sally. You just spent it," Mary explained.

Sally knew Mary was right. She had spent almost all of her money. Sure it was kind of fun, but now she hardly had anything left.

"Money sure goes fast."

Chapter Six
The Penny Plan Budget

Money does go fast, if you're not watching where it's going. Isn't it easy to spend money like Sally, when you're not thinking about how much you're spending or why? Have you ever bought something on a whim, only to get home and realize that you sure spent a lot of money on something you didn't really need, or even want that much? Well, there are two things you can do to end that problem, think before you spend (see Chapter Eight) and create a budget. The purpose of a budget is to help you control your spending habits so that you can make the most of what you have, as well as to save more effectively for your future goals. Remember that when you save money it's like paying yourself. So give yourself a raise by creating a budget. It will help you spend less on unnecessary things and more for investing in your future because that's what your savings are, an investment in your future.

A budget helps you analyze how you should divide your money, considering how much you make. The next step is to then to try to stick within *your own* limits. Everyone's budget is going to be different because everyone makes a different amount of money, has different opinions on how that money should be spent, and has different values of importance. One person may allot more of his money for the savings category because he's trying to save for college, but another person might allot more money for the leisure category because he likes going to the movies every week.

In order to make a budget, you first have to get an idea of approximately how much money you will make in an average month. If you have a steady job and work about the same amount of hours every week, simply take one of your checks and multiply it by four (if you get paid weekly). If you get paid every two weeks, multiply it by two, etc. Some months have more than four weeks, but it is better to *underestimate* how much you will make. This way you usually won't get stuck with less money than what you expect. The good side is that some months you will make more money than what you expect. If you do odd jobs and don't get a set amount every month, then estimate about how much you normally make based on past months. Again, underestimate the amount. You do not want to wind up with less money than what you planned on having.

Now that you have an approximation of how much you will make monthly, you need to consider what you spend that money on. Below is a worksheet you can use to list some of the things you spend your money on, followed by an example that may help you out.

Where My Money Goes

_____

_____

_____

_____

_____

_____

_____

_____

_____

_____

_____

_____

_____

_____

_____

_____

Examples of Where Your Money Might Go

1. Food

2. Clothes

3. Personal items (girls might buy make-up, guys might pay to get a haircut)

4. Leisure (going out and doing things you like)

5. Gifts (to charity groups, as well as to friends and family)

6. Church Offering

7. Gas

8. Car insurance

9. Car maintenance and repairs

If you have a lot of similar categories, try to combine some of them to form a total of seven, or fewer, general categories. It will make things a little bit easier for our next few exercises. For example, I combined all automobile categories (car insurance, maintenance, repairs, and gas) and titled it "Car." I also combined church offering, charitable gifts, and family gifts into one category, "Gifts." I then included four additional independent categories: "Clothing," "Personal," "Food," and "Leisure." Finally, because inevitably there will be things that do not fit into any of these categories, there must be one category for "Other." List your simplified categories below. (You may want to use the same ones as I did.)

1.

2.

3.

4.

5.

6.

7.

Now that you have simplified the categories in which you spend your money, it's time to apply the penny plan budget.

The Penny Plan Budget

What you will need:

- Lots of spare change
- Paper
- Pencil

What to do:

1) Write each category of expenditure from page 71 on a separate sheet of paper and spread the papers out on a floor or table.

2) Add a category for savings.

3) Use the change to represent your monthly earnings. Each penny equals one dollar, so count out enough pennies, and maybe some dimes, nickels, and quarters, to equal your monthly income. Put all extra coins aside for the time being.

   Formula: 1¢ = $1

                    5¢ = $5

                   10¢ = $10

                   25¢ = $25

4) Start with the savings category and put enough change in that pile to represent how much you would like to save per month.

5) Use the remaining change to determine how to allocate your income in the other categories.

6) If you run out of change before allocating resources to each category, this means you will need to cut costs somewhere. Try to cut the budget in another category to provide change for your remaining categories.

7) Once you have divided up all of the money, do a final count for how much you can spend in each area, and write it down on the paper for each category.

Alternative: Pie Chart Method

If you don't have a lot of change at home, use the circle below to make an approximate pie graph of how you want to divide your money. Start with the savings category. Set a goal for how much you want to save and then work the rest of your budget around that. Use the example to help you.

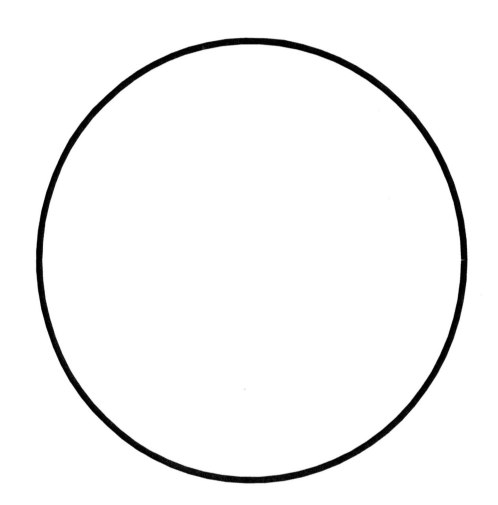

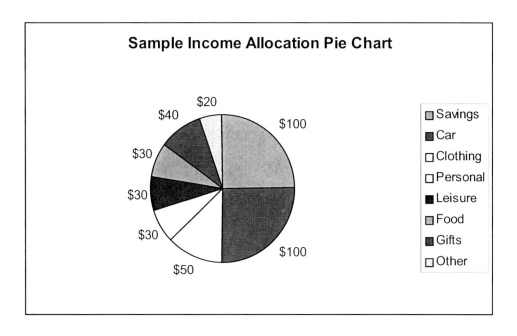

Now use the numbers you came up with in the Penny Plan Budget or with the Pie Chart Method to write out your budget in list form. An example is shown below.

Estimated Monthly Budget

Income	$400

Expenditures:

1. Savings	$100
2. Car	$100
3. Personal	$30
4. Clothing	$50
5. Leisure	$30
6. Food	$30
7. Gifts	$40
8. Other	$20
	Total: $400

Now that you've considered what you make, what you spend your money on, and how much you think you should allow yourself in each category, you have to put your budget to the test. For the next few months I want you to keep track of every penny you spend. This will show how you *really* spend your money. You might think you can only afford to save $55 a month, but maybe by the end of the month you'll manage to save $70. Maybe you budgeted $50 for leisure, but found you only spent $30. Tracking your expenditures for the next month will give you clues on how to revise your budget so that it works for you. It will also indicate problem areas, where you may be spending too much. So how should you keep track of all the money you make, spend, and save? Make a chart using the steps below. (I have included some blank charts in the back of this book, but it is good to know how to make them yourself, too. There is also an example on the following page you can use to help you.) After you finish tracking your money for a month, use the instructions given to determine how to evaluate your results.

How to Keep Track of the Money You Make, Save, and Spend

Note: Use a spreadsheet program on a computer if you have access to one.

1. Create a header to show the month for which you will be tracking your money. Example: July 2001 Expenditures
2. List all of the dates (for the month) down the leftmost column.
3. Make a column for each of the categories you listed in your budget. (This is why we combined categories. It might be difficult to fit ten to fifteen columns on one page.)
4. Make a column labeled "Income" to record all of your earnings.

3

July 2001 Expenditures

Date	Car	Personal	Clothing	Leisure	Food	Gifts	Other	Income
7/1/01								
7/2/01								
7/3/01								
7/4/01					6.17			
7/5/01								
7/6/01								92.68
7/7/01			30.69					
7/8/01						10.00		
7/9/01	12.00							
7/10/01				5.50				
7/11/01					3.54			
7/12/01		3.49						
7/13/01								102.25
7/14/01					4.22			
7/15/01						10.00		
7/16/01								
7/17/01	85.00						6.40	
7/18/01								
7/19/01								
7/20/01					5.62			95.62
7/21/01								
7/22/01		6.77		5.50		10.00		
7/23/01								
7/24/01								
7/25/01					1.05			
7/26/01								
7/27/01								110.26
7/28/01								
7/29/01	15.00					10.00		
7/30/01					7.85			
7/31/01								
Budgeted	100.00	30.00	50.00	30.00	30.00	40.00	20.00	400.00
Totals	112.00	10.26	30.69	11.00	28.45	40.00	6.40	400.81
Difference	-12.00	19.74	19.31	19.00	1.55	0.00	13.60	-0.81
Ttl.Income	400.81							
Ttl. Spent	238.80							
Ttl. Saved	162.01							

How to Use Your Chart

1. Every time you spend money on something, locate where the column of the appropriate category and the row of the date that you spent the money on meet. Then, write in the amount you spent.

2. Under each column, write the amount you budgeted for that category. (See example on the previous page.)

3. At the end of the month, add up the amount spent in each column. Write each amount spent underneath the amount budgeted. The sum under the "Income" column indicates the total amount you earned throughout the month.

4. Subtract the total amount that you spent in each category from the amount that you budgeted for that category. This is how much you deviated from your budget. If the answer is positive, you remained within your budget. If your answer is negative, that means you overspent.

   ***Note:** If you overspent in some categories and under-spent in others, check out how you did overall. Was the total of all your expenditures more or less than what you planned on? It's okay to deviate from your budget a little bit, but it is a good idea to stick within the broad limit of your expenditures. For example, if you were over budget on food by $10, but under budget on leisure by $20, overall you're still $10 under budget for those two categories combined. ***

5. Include three additional rows to summarize your total income, total amount spent, and total savings. The total income was already calculated, but you will have to add each of the category totals to determine your total spending for the month. Subtract your total spending from your total income in order to determine your total savings.

6. As a check on your work, look at your bank statement for the month and see if your calculated savings are in line with the increase in your bank balance. Of course there will probably be some error, but if your figures seem really off, add up all the columns again and double check your work. Also make sure you don't forget to record anything because that will throw your figures off, too.

7. Examine how you spent your money and revise your budget as necessary.

Tracking your expenditures for a month might surprise you. You may never have realized how much you spent on fast food or clothes. Keeping track of your money might also help you think more about how you're spending it. This exercise is especially important in creating an effective budget, but it's a good idea to continue the process of recording your expenditures simply to keep a check on where all of your money is going.

TIPS for You and Your Budget

1) **Keep your table of expenditures in a handy place**, where it won't be a burden to record your data every day. I keep mine magneted to my closet. Maybe your closet isn't magnetic, but you can post it on a corkboard or tape it somewhere. I don't recommend putting it in your file, where you would have to pull it out all of the time. Don't put it into your file until the entire table is complete.

2) **Be realistic.** Don't budget $10 a month for gas if you know you will need to spend about $30. You can't alter your needs, but you can limit spending on your wants.

3) **Try to remain within a certain limit of *total* spending**. If you overspend in one category, try to under-spend in another so that overall you don't exceed your total budget.

4) **Keep your budget updated.** This is another good reason to keep track of your expenditures continually. Your circumstances and your spending habits *will* change, and when they do, so should your budget.

5) **Don't stick to the *usual* budget for an *unusual* circumstance**. Some months may require more spending, for example in December you might have many Christmas presents to buy. You didn't plan your budget with Christmas in mind, so don't rely on it. Instead, make a list of approximately how much you can afford to spend on each person and try to stick within your new limits.

6) Save the extra money. If you make more money than what you estimated, follow your budget as planned and save all of the extra money. For more tips on saving, read on to the next chapter.

Additional Resources

Books

Money Management Using Excel
By L. Louis Van Osdol

Kits

The Budget Kit, monthly planner
Dearborn Financial Publishing
$15.95 + $4.00 shipping and handling
1-800-283-4380

Personal Budget Planner
Career Advancement Center
$19.95 + $3.00 shipping and handling
1-800-295-1325

BECOMING MONEY-WISE:

MILKING YOUR MONEY

Fred Forgets

"So, what did you get Mom for her birthday, Fred?"

"Oh, no! I forgot."

"It's in three days. I can't believe you forgot."

"Man," Fred groaned, "I've already spent all of my money for the week, and I won't get paid again until the day after mom's birthday."

"You could always make her something," Brandon suggested.

"I don't know. I'm not too crafty. I'm just going to have to find a way to earn some money before her birthday rolls around." Fred pondered, "Maybe I could mow a few lawns. Wanna help me?"

"I don't think so, Fred. It's gotta be a hundred degrees out. You should have been a more thoughtful son, like me," Brandon bragged. "I'm not the one who went and forgot her birthday, so you can battle the heat alone, brother."

Fred didn't like the idea of mowing lawns in hundred degree weather, but at least it wouldn't be difficult to find business. No one else wants to mow their lawn in that kind of weather either. So Fred went out and mowed two lawns. That was all he could take. The sun and the heat had just exhausted him. He had $25.

"I guess I can get her some flowers and balloons with this," Fred said. "If only I had kept a little money saved up. Then I wouldn't have had to mow those lawns in this weather."

"That's what you get, smart boy!"

Chapter Seven
Saving Your Money

Saving is a very important aspect of money management. If you're making money, you should be saving money, even if there is absolutely no specific purpose for saving it. You should always have money saved up for an emergency or an unexpected event. If you have a car, you never know when you'll need a repair. You also could wind up in Fred's situation, with a birthday around the corner and no resources to prepare for it, or you might just see something you really like that's only on sale for another week.

In the last chapter you developed a budget and one of the categories you budgeted for was "Savings." So how much should you save? You should try to save at least 10%, but aim for as high as you can. When I started my first job, my initial savings goal was 50%, and since I didn't have a car yet, I actually achieved it. Whatever your goal is, make sure it's feasible. If you plan on saving 75% of your wages and never manage to do it, you'll begin to disregard your goal. So over-setting your goal is almost as bad as not setting one at all.

So where are you going to stash the money you're saving? Hopefully not at home in your secret spot. You shouldn't put the money you save anywhere that you have easy access to it, because it might not be saved for very long. For example, let's say Fred did start saving and he kept all of the money he saved in a shoebox. When Saturday night rolls around, he only has $5 and wants a little bit more to go out. He decides to take an extra $15 out of his shoe box. Pretty soon there is nothing left in his shoe box because all of the money he has "saved" has been spent. This is why it is a good idea to open a savings account. You can always withdraw, or take money out, when you need to, but somehow, because it's not quite as simple as pulling it out of your shoe box, you're less likely to withdraw money for petty purposes.

Another advantage is that you earn interest. So while your money is sitting in the bank, the bank is paying you for letting them use it. Typically, this is only about 0-3%, but depending on how much money you have, the interest you earn could be quite significant. Regardless, a little bit of money here and a little bit of money there can add up to a lot of money. Why refuse 3% interest by keeping your money at home, where it could get lost or stolen? Another advantage to having a savings account is that most are insured by the FDIC (Federal Deposit Insurance Corporation) or NCUA (National Credit Union Administration). This means that if for some reason the bank can't give you your money, the federal government will, for up to $100,000. However, realistically if you had a lot of money owed to you, it might take some time to get it all back, but the fact is: you will get it back eventually, which is better than never at all.

How to Open a Savings Account

1. <u>Save the Money</u>

   Many banks charge a "fall-below fee" for having less than the required amount, usually about $200, in an account. Many banks also require as little as $5 to open an account, but because this is less than $200, you'll be paying the fee. With this in mind, don't plan on opening an account until you accumulate $200 first. Don't get the shoe box-syndrome, though. Try to keep the money you save saved! Keep it out of reach if you can.

2. <u>Shop around.</u>

a) Check out which banks are federally insured. Most banks that are FDIC insured display an "FDIC" label on their doors so that their customers know they are protected. If you don't see it, it probably isn't insured, but ask someone who works at the bank. If it's a credit union, check if it's NCUA insured.

b) Check out the interest rates. Not all banks offer the same rate. One might offer 2%. Another might offer 3%. You may not think a 1% difference is very much, but more is more, and as your money grows, it will be significant.

c) See what benefits each bank offers. What are the bank's hours? Try to find the bank with the most flexible hours for you. Check out if there are any free gifts involved in joining a bank or credit union, but don't base your decision on one free gift.

d) Beware of extra fees. As mentioned above, many banks charge a fee for falling below a certain minimum balance. Many banks, however, wave this fee for minors. Find out which banks do and which banks don't. (Maybe you won't have to wait to save up $200 first after all.) Be on the lookout for fees of any kind and determine how they would affect you.

e) Talk to relatives and other adults about what bank they go to and why. Chances are good that you'll wind up going to the same bank as your parents. Your parents probably have some good reasons for going there, but ask other people so you can get the full scope of your options.

f) Consider the location of the bank. You don't want to have to drive twenty miles every time you need some money.

3. <u>Go to the bank and do it.</u>

a) Don't wait in line to talk to one of the bank tellers. They only deal with routine functions (that you will soon be a part of), and will only give you someone else to talk to. Of course if you're really unsure about where to go, ask one of the bank tellers or someone else that works there.

b) Usually there is a separate section of the bank that handles opening new accounts and granting loans. Tell someone in that area of the bank that you want to open a Regular Savings Account. The people at the bank will most likely be very accommodating and will explain everything that you have to do. Basically, you just have to fill out a form, identify yourself, and have an initial deposit.

Once you have your own bank account, you'll need to know how to make deposits and withdrawals. To deposit simply means to put money into your bank account. [You might want to talk to your employer about direct deposit in which you can have all or part of your check automatically deposited into your savings account. If he or she approves, usually you will just have to fill out a simple form to get it set up.] To withdraw means to take money out of your bank account. All banks do things differently, but most have two separate slips for making deposits and withdrawals. Each bank will also have a different layout, but they'll mainly want the same information, which includes your account number, your name, how much money you want to put into the bank or take out, what type of account you have, and sometimes your address. The basic directions for filling out a deposit slip are shown on the next few pages, followed by two examples.

Filling Out a Deposit Slip

1. Write your name at the top, where it says "Account Name."

2. Fill in your account number below.

3. Write the date in the top right corner next to "Date."

4. Enter how much cash you are depositing on the line next to "Cash."
   ***Note:** If you are not depositing any cash, leave this line blank. ***

5. Write down each check you are depositing separately on the lines next to where it says "Checks." For example, if you were depositing two checks, write down the amount of the first check and then write down the amount of the second check below that.
   Note:** If you are not depositing any checks, leave these lines blank.

6. Where it says "Total," add up all cash and checks that you are depositing.

7. Where it says "Less Cash Received," write down how much cash you would like to receive back. For example, if you were depositing a check for $100 and you wanted $20 in cash back, you would write $20.
   ***Note:** If you do not want any cash back, leave this line blank. ***

8. Subtract the cash you want to receive back (the amount next to "Less Cash Received") from the total. This is your "Net Deposit."
   ***Note:** If you did not want any cash back your "Total" will be equal to your "Net Deposit." ***

Example 1: Frederick has a check for $100 and he wants to keep $25 and put $75 in the bank. After filling out the basic information, he writes $100.00 next to "Total of All Checks," $100.00 next to "Total," and $25.00 next to "Less Cash Received." Finally, he writes $75 next to "Net Deposit."

Community Bank

Savings Deposit

Date: 7/06/01

Account Name	Cash	$
		100.00
Frederick Stanley	Checks	
Account Number	Total	100.00
	Less Cash Received	25.00
3 2 6 9 5 3 2	Net Deposit	$ 75.00

Example 2: Frederick has saved up $45.00 and he has two checks, one for $20.00 and one for $36.73. He wants to put all of it in the bank. Again, he fills out the basic information and then writes $45.00 next to "Cash," $20 on one line and $36.73 on the next by "Checks," and $101.73 next to "Total." He leaves "Less Cash Received" blank and writes $101.73 next to "Net Deposit."

Community Bank

Savings Deposit

Date: 7/6/01

Account Name	Cash	$ 45.00
		20.00
Frederick Stanley	Checks	36.73
Account Number	Total	101.73
	Less Cash Received	
3 2 6 9 5 3 2	Net Deposit	$ 101.73

Filling out a withdrawal slip is very similar to filling out a deposit slip. Simply write your name and the date, sign your name, write the amount you want to withdraw, and write your account number. Leave the bottom, where it says "Bank Use Only" blank. Below is a blank withdrawal slip you can fill out using the example.

Community Bank		Savings Withdrawal
		Date

Account Name (*Please Print*)	Dollar Amount
	$
Signature	Account No.

Bank Use Only	Initials	ID	Disposition	890 = Regular 534 = Closing	TC

Community Bank		Savings Withdrawal
		Date 7/6/01

Account Name (*Please Print*) Frederick Stanley	Dollar Amount $ 40.00
Signature Frederick P. Stanley	Account No. 3 2 6 9 5 3 2

Bank Use Only	Initials	ID	Disposition	890 = Regular 534 = Closing	TC

Every month, or quarter, your bank should mail you a statement containing information about your account. Banks that send statements quarterly often print them at the end of March, June, September, and December. You should receive them within a couple weeks after each quarter. The statement will show your balance at the beginning of the quarter, all withdrawals and deposits throughout the quarter, the interest you have earned, and your new balance. It lists the dates, description, amount, and new balance for each transaction so you can get an overview of your bank activity and make sure that there haven't been any mistakes. An example of a bank statement is shown on the following page.

National Bank

22000 West Park Boulevard
Pine Lake, MI 48256
(810) 555-2200

CAMERON M. LILLEY
OR SAMANTHA L. LILLEY
55513 WILLOW
PINE LAKE, MI 48256-2321

TO REPORT ERRORS OR MAKE INQUIRIES
ABOUT LOANS, WRITE:
SUPERVISORY COMMITTEE CHAIRMAN
POSTOFFICE BOX 4444
PINE LAKE, MI 48256

STATEMENT OF ACCOUNT	PAGE	STATEMENT FROM	STATEMENT THRU	ACCOUNT NUMBER
	1	04/08/01	07/10/01	525264-3

DATE	DESCRIPTION OF TRANSACTION	AMOUNT	BALANCE
4/8/01	PREVIOUS BALANCE		201.47
4/10/01	DEPOSIT	46.00	247.47
4/13/01	WITHDRAWAL	-15.00	232.47
4/17/01	DEPOSIT	50.00	282.47
4/24/01	DEPOSIT	42.39	324.86
5/1/01	DEPOSIT	50.00	374.86
5/8/01	DEPOSIT	45.00	419.86
5/11/01	WITHDRAWAL	-20.00	399.86
5/15/01	DEPOSIT	62.58	462.44
5/22/01	DEPOSIT	59.45	521.89
5/29/01	DEPOSIT	40.00	561.89
6/5/01	WITHDRAWAL	-100.00	461.89
6/12/01	DEPOSIT	48.65	510.54
6/19/01	DEPOSIT	102.56	613.10
6/26/01	DEPOSIT	101.15	714.25
6/30/01	INTEREST FOR REGULAR SAVINGS ACCOUNT	2.14	716.39
7/3/01	DEPOSIT	80.00	796.39
7/10/01	DEPOSIT	98.26	894.65
7/10/01	NEW BALANCE		894.65

INTEREST PERIOD: 4/1/01 THRU 6/30/01
INTEREST RATE: 2.5%
INTEREST PAID AND CREDITED: CURRENT $2.14
YTD: $4.02

Savings Bonds

There are several ways to save in addition to savings accounts and many pay more interest. Another way to save is with federal savings bonds. Savings bonds can be bought at your bank by simply filling out a form indicating what bonds you want to buy and also some basic personal information, such as your name, address, and social security number. Savings bonds can also be purchased directly from http://www.usbonds.gov. Within two weeks after you've filled out the form, you will receive the actual bonds in the mail. Bonds can be bought for a variety of prices. There are $50, $500, $1000, etc., but is that how much they cost? No. Each bond costs exactly half of what it says. A $50 bond would cost $25. It is called a $50 bond, though, because that is how much it will be worth when it matures. Maturity simply means how long it will take to reach its stated value. Today, it takes about seventeen years, but that number is subject to change. Seventeen years sounds like a long time, however, you would still be making slightly more interest than you would from a savings account.

***Note: The interest rate is set every six months, in the months of May and November. To find out the current rate, call 1-800-US-BONDS. ***

Another advantage to buying savings bonds is that they can be stored away so that you don't spend them as easily, but you can cash them at any time after the first six months if you should ever need the money. Be careful when you cash them, though, because the interest only accumulates on the first day of every month. So if you want to redeem a bond on May 31st, you won't receive any of the interest for the month of May, but if you wait until June 1st you will get the full interest you deserve. Also keep in mind that there is a three-month interest penalty for bonds cashed in before five years. So if you hold a bond for one year and then cash it in, you will only receive nine months worth of interest. For this reason, savings bonds should only be purchased if you are planning on holding them for a long time. Another thing you should be aware of is that after your bond reaches its maturity and it's worth the face value you can continue to gain interest on it, but after thirty years your bond will stop gaining interest. So, if you ever buy savings bonds for the long-term, don't keep them any longer than thirty years.

Certificates of Deposit (C.D.)

One of the best savings options for teenagers is the certificate of deposit. A certificate of deposit is simply a contract between you and the bank. It's essentially like giving the bank a loan. You let them use a certain amount of your money for a specified amount of time, and then when the time is up you get your money back plus the interest the bank paid you for letting them use it. The interest you earn on these is usually more than the interest you would earn from a regular savings account or bonds, but it varies. Typical rates are often between 2% and 7% yearly. Many certificates of deposit require at least $500 for a minimum of six months. However, often times as the minimum amount of money and amount of time go up the more interest you can earn. Shop around for the best rates. Different banks have different plans, and even within a single bank one plan may be more beneficial to you than another.

You also want to consider the amount of time that you are willing to give up your money for. For example, a five-year certificate of deposit might pay more interest, but if you plan on buying a car and needing the money before then, this wouldn't be a good option. You can withdraw the money from a C.D. (certificate of deposit) early, but you will be penalized. A typical penalty might be the loss of three months' interest, but it will vary from bank to bank.

Certificates of deposit are a good option for you if you have enough money to get one and you can afford to part with the money for a while. The fact that certificates of deposit discourage against early withdrawal makes it one of your best options. Once you put your money in, you don't have the freedom to withdraw it as easily as you can with a regular savings account or bonds, so you are more likely to keep the money saved. Nevertheless, you should always keep some money in your savings account, in case of an emergency, to avoid having to withdraw your C.D. early. In other words, don't put *all* of your money in a C.D.

Opening a C.D. is quite simple. Once you decide what C.D. plan you want, go to the bank and tell them. As with opening any account, the people at the bank will be very helpful.

Money Market Accounts

A money market account is a savings account in which you must maintain a higher minimum balance than would normally be required for a regular savings account, but you earn a higher interest rate than with a regular savings account. For example, a typical minimum balance for a savings account may be $200, while the minimum balance for a money market account may be $2500.

One advantage of a money market account over a certificate of deposit is that you can withdraw money without penalty, as long as you maintain the minimum balance. However, a certificate of deposit may offer a higher rate. Overall, a money market account can be a good option if you want to earn higher rates and still have the flexibility of withdrawing your money. Of course it may take a while to earn enough to meet the minimum balance requirement.

Mutual Funds

A mutual fund is a pool of investments managed by a professional portfolio manager, made available to the investing public. They come in many shapes and forms. Some are low-risk investments that invest in short-term government bonds and others are high-risk investments that invest in aggressive stocks or concentrated sectors of the market, like technology. Some mutual funds are actively managed and others are managed passively to mirror a specified index. Because there is a lot of information that must be understood before investing in a mutual fund, investors must be at least eighteen years old and must have read the prospectus. A prospectus is simply a booklet of information concerning an investment that allows the investor to make an informed decision. Although this may sound complicated, there are a lot of advantages to mutual funds.

Many people like mutual funds because they are managed by highly trained individuals and can allow for greater diversification. For example, a stock mutual fund may consist of stock in over one hundred different companies. An investor can invest $1000 in that fund, simply by filling out a quick form and mailing a check, and achieve the benefits of owning a small piece of each of the stocks owned by the fund. This allows the investor to avoid the risk of investing all of his money in one stock. In other words, mutual funds allow investors to diversify, which means to spread out risk, with small amounts of money. Keep in mind, though, that mutual funds are not federally insured. There is no guarantee that you will not lose your money. However, there are many mutual funds, such as Money Market Mutual Funds, that only invest in very safe reliable investments, and often are very stable. Also be aware that many mutual funds charge a fee for your investment, but for a list of 100% *no-load* mutual funds, meaning it won't cost you any extra fees to invest in them, request one from the address given on the "Additional Resource" page at the end of this chapter.

These five options, opening a regular savings account, buying federal savings bonds, investing in certificates of deposit, opening a money market account, and investing in a mutual fund will probably be the most useful for you. There are still many other ways to save your money such as with stocks and other types of bonds. You may want to utilize these as well, once you feel you have a good understanding of them. Check the "Additional Resources" page at the end of this chapter for more information.

TIPS for Saving a Bundle

1) **Save first. Spend Later.** Put the money for *you* in the bank before it gets spent on something else. A good way to do this is to go to the bank once each time you get your paycheck and only take what you *need*, save the rest, and don't go back until your next paycheck.

2) **Constantly set financial goals for yourself and reach them.** For example, set a goal to save $100 a month and do it.

3) **Don't carry around a lot of cash**, especially if you don't need it for anything specific. Money that you put in your pocket will most likely get spent.

4) **Throw all of your loose change in a bank or in a container and roll it at the end of each month.**

5) **Know the Rule of 72's.** To find out how many years it will take your money to double, divide 72 by the interest rate. For example, if you are earning 8% interest, it will take 9 years for your money to double ($72/8 = 9$).

6) **Eat at home instead of going out for food or pack a lunch instead of buying at school.**

7) **Drink water at a restaurant as opposed to paying for a soda.**

8) **Consider buying videos and compact discs used or check them out from the library for free.** The library may not have everything, but you would probably be surprised by what they do have.

9) **Make a list of things you can cut back on and save the extra money.**

Additional Resources

Books for Investing in Mutual Funds and Stocks

The Guide to Investing in Mutual Funds
By: David L. Scott
$8.95

Business Week Guide to Mutual Funds
$14.95

Money Guide: The Stock Market
By the editors of "Money"
$6.95

Free Information

One Hundred Percent No-Load Mutual Fund Council
1501 Broadway
Suite 312
New York, NY 10036
212-768-2477
(for a list of mutual funds that don't charge extra money to invest)

"U.S. Savings Bond" free information
Bureau of Public Debt
1300 C Street SW
Washington, DC 20239

Phone Numbers

1-800-US-BONDS   A recording will tell you the current rates

Websites

http://www.savingsbonds.gov

http://www.fidelity.com

http://www.vanguard.com

A Giving Experience

"How are we supposed to give other people money when we don't even have our own money?" Joey complained.

"First of all you wouldn't be giving anyone *money.* You would be using your money to give to people less fortunate than yourself," Dad explained. "How would you like it if one Christmas morning you woke up and there were no presents for you because your mother and I couldn't afford it?"

"Let Santa come through," Joey laughed. "Anyway, I still don't have any money."

"Well, that's another thing, Joey. You're mother and I have been thinking that it's time to start giving you and Annie an allowance."

"An allowance!!!! We're richhhhhh!!!" the children exclaimed.

"Calm down you two. We are not just going to give you money. You're going to have to earn it." Mother proclaimed.

"Oh, great. What do we have to do now?" Annie groaned.

"Well, first, you have to decide what jobs you will do around the house to earn an allowance. Here's the list of all the jobs you can do and how much each job pays." Mother handed them each a full sheet of paper with writing from top to bottom. Joey and Annie's eyes bulged as they scanned the list.

"The first one to turn their list in gets first pick if any jobs conflict. Then, after that you're going to have to develop a budget. I want to see a list of how you plan to spend your money, and then I want you to stick to it. Got it?" Mother answered.

"Oh, yeah, and don't forget. Your rooms are not an option. They must remain clean, but we will pay you $5 a week for keeping them clean.

However, for every day that their messy, you lose a dollar of your allowance," Dad added.

"So go to it kids."

About an hour later Joey and Annie came back. Neither of them was ready to do any jobs daily, so they each chose one weekly job. Joey decided he would clean the living room once a week (including dusting, vacuuming, etc.). Annie decided she would clean the bathroom once a week. Each was about an hour job, so they would be paid $5 for each job plus $5 for keeping their rooms clean for a total of $10 a week. So now they had to develop a budget.

"Mom, what kind of things should we include in our budget?" Annie asked.

"Well, have you decided if you want to contribute any money to help the neighbors down the street? You do realize that they don't have a lot of money and their children probably won't get hardly any toys for Christmas. And if you do decide to help, you can't tell anyone."

"Why not?"

"Well, Annie. Sometimes it's important to do nice things for other people, but you have to make sure you're doing it for the right reasons. You should help another person because you want to, not because you think you'll look nice and generous if you do. Telling people is kind of like showing off your generosity."

Annie kind of liked this secret idea. It would be a secret mission. And imagine how happy they would be. "Sure Mom. I'll help, but what else should I consider in my budget?"

"Well, you should start saving money for yourself, too. One day you'll probably want to buy a car and house and all kinds of things. Maybe there's something you really want now that you want to save for, like a new stereo."

"Yeah, a new stereo! That would be cool!"

So Joey and Annie went to work on their budgets.

"Are you really going to contribute some of your money to give to those kids for Christmas, Annie?"

"Well, Joey. Wouldn't you be sad if you didn't get any presents on Christmas?"

"I guess I would. How much are you going to give?"

"I think I'm going to give a dollar a week."

"Yeah, I guess I'll give a dollar a week, too," Joey finally gave in after feeling a little left out—everyone else was helping.

*   *   *   *   *

"You guys about done?" Mom yelled from the living room.

"Yeah," the kids jogged in excitedly. "We just finished."

"Well, let's see 'em kids," Dad was really interested now to see how his kids planned on spending their money.

"Can I go first?" Annie asked anxiously.

"Sure go ahead."

"I'm going to save $1 a week for Christmas presents for the neighbors, which will be $12 by Christmas. I'm going to save three dollars a week, which will be $36 by Christmas. And then I'll have six dollars left to spend every week. What's your budget Joey?"

"I'm going to save $1 a week for the neighbors, too."

"That's great, Joey! We're really glad you came around," Dad interrupted.

"I'm not finished yet. I'm also going to save $2 a week, and have $7 left to spend."

"Okay, kids. I think you made really good decisions. You'll start your chores next Saturday, and we'll pay you right after you finish. Remember to stick to your budgets," Mother finished the family meeting.

"Aren't you proud of them Maggie. They're really learning responsibility, generosity, and organization. I really think it was a great idea of yours to remember the Christmas spirit and think of such a beautiful thing our family can do."

"Thanks, honey. It's getting late. Let's go to bed."

*   *   *   *   *

It was a week before Christmas and the family was going shopping for presents to give to the neighbors' children.

"Okay, I want each one of you to go and pick out three presents. Joey, you pick out presents for Tommy, and Annie, you can pick out presents for Sarah. I know they're younger than you guys are, so try and think of what things you liked when you were their age," Mother explained.

Joey picked out a set of action figures, a set of walkie talkies, and a set of baseball cards. Annie picked out a talking doll, a tea set, and a barbie doll. The children were so excited because they knew Tommy and Sarah were going to love their gifts. In the meantime, their parents were also picking out wonderful gifts for them.

*   *   *   *   *

Finally, the time had come. It was Christmas Eve. The family had spent the whole day wrapping each other's presents and presents for their neighbors. It was four o'clock in the morning, the perfect time to drop off the presents without anyone seeing. The kids were so excited they begged to go too, so when their parents woke them up they didn't even complain. They jumped right up. They packed all of the presents into large garbage bags, walked down the block (so as not to make any noise shutting car doors or anything), carefully placed the bags on the front porch, and walked back home. Everyone was so excited, imagining what the neighbors' reaction would be. The family decided that since this Christmas idea was such a success that every year they would make one goal that would preserve the Christmas spirit.

The end.

Even though Annie and Joey were reluctant to part with their money at first, their decision to share with their less fortunate neighbors turned out to be a very exciting and rewarding experience. Everyone should plan on sharing at least some of their money with others, so make giving a part of your budget and your spending habits. The next chapter will help you learn how to spend wisely, but to remember not to be stingy. It will also give you some ideas on how *you* can share your money. Here's one you can start with now: Secretly buy, or make, something for someone having a bad day or for someone who is in a less fortunate situation.

Chapter Eight
Spending and Sharing

We all spend money, but how we spend it varies for everyone. We have already talked about how to budget the money we spend, but there are smart ways of spending that money that will help you still get the things that you want without wasting too much money. When you want to buy something there are some important steps you should take before making the actual purchase:

1. **Think about it.** Do you really need it? If you don't need it, why do you want it? Compare the costs with the benefits. Is the price worth the benefit the product will give you?

2. **Shop around.** Find the best price. Look for specials and sales in ads, newspapers, or just by going to different stores.

3. **Make the decision, using the above tactics, but <u>take your time</u>.** Don't buy anything on the spur of the moment. Often when things are bought without consideration it is soon discovered that you could have gotten it for less money or that you didn't really need it in the first place.

If you are out shopping at a mall and you see something you really think you want, don't buy it right away. Instead plan on swinging by right before you leave and if you haven't seen it at another store for a lower price, found anything else you wanted more, and still think you really want to buy it, go for it. Waiting until before you leave to make the actual purchase gives you some time to really consider it first, and it saves you from having to carry it around for the rest of the day.

If you want to buy something of considerable value (a stereo or a new bike), definitely consider it for at least a week. Talk to friends and relatives about the product. Don't forget that quality counts, too. You don't want to buy a certain brand simply because it's the cheapest. You want to buy the product that has the quality you want for a price worthwhile. You can check up on a specific product or brand in magazines such as "Consumer Reports," which rate and evaluate various products.

Use the above three steps (think about it, shop around, and take your time) before you buy anything. Don't worry. These steps don't have to take a long time. For example, answer question number one first, "Do you need it?" If you do, you have to buy it, but should you necessarily buy it from the first place you see it? No. If you already know the average price of what it is you want to buy, it may be easy to tell if it's a good price or not. If you consider it a good price, buy it. If not, go somewhere else. However, if the alternate place to buy the product from is too far away or inconvenient, you may be better off to pay the extra cost. For example, if I was at a store and the pencils I needed seemed a little expensive, it would probably be simpler to buy the pencils there anyway because the difference in the price of pencils cannot be great enough to be worth the gas money and the trip to get them somewhere else.

If the product is simply something you want, then it will require a little more thinking. When you need something, you know you have to buy it, you just have to try to find a good price. If it's something you want, you first have to decide if it is worth buying and then try to find the best price. A good way to decide if it is worth buying is to compare the cost of the product with how many hours of work it would take you to pay for it. Do you really want to work that long for the product? For example, if there was a pair of $65 jeans you liked and you made $6 an hour, it would take you about 11 hours to pay for them—actually more considering that after taxes are taken out you do not make a full $6 for each hour of work. You decide that you do want to buy a pair of jeans, but you are not sure if it's worth 11 hours of work. Then, you see a pair of jeans that only costs $25, which would only take about 4 hours of work to pay for. So are the $65 jeans worth enough to you that you want to spend an extra 7 hours of work for them? This is a good way of looking at things before you decide whether or not you want to buy something.

Tipping

Whenever you go to a restaurant, get your haircut, or have a service done for you (ex. have a bellhop carry your bags, have a taxi drive you somewhere) you should leave a tip. It is standard to give 15%, but that can be higher or lower depending on what kind of service you get. If you go to a restaurant and you have a very good waitress, you may want to leave a bigger tip. After all, waitresses often have to rely on their tips for income because their hourly wage is very low. If, however, you receive very poor service you should not feel guilty about reducing your tip or even completely not leaving one, which you should only do in a situation of extremely terrible service. Keep in mind, though, what the waitress is responsible for. For example, if you didn't like the food, that's not really the waitress' fault, so don't penalize her tip. Leave your tip based solely on the service provided.

Giving

You should focus some of your money on giving. If you go to church, set a goal of how much to give each week or each month, or set a percentage of your pay that you would like to give. (Usually 10% is a good amount.) If you do not go to church, contribute to other foundations, such as those that battle diseases like cancer, pledge money or buy something for a fundraiser, buy a gift for a family member, take a friend to lunch, or give to other charitable foundations. The point is that you want to spend your money *wisely*, and spending it wisely means sharing it with others. You should be conscious of where your money is going and careful about how you spend it, but giving is always a worthy investment. However, don't give more than you can afford to. You too have needs that must be met.

You should also be careful about whom you give your money to. Churches and people that you know well are usually pretty safe, but be aware of associations that you are not familiar with. Don't give your money freely if you are not sure where it will go. If you have ever received a request for a donation from some type of foundation in the mail, you can't really be sure if the foundation is legit. You don't know the people in charge of that foundation personally, so how can you really know where your money will go? Well, let's say it's a foundation for cancer research and your grandpa has cancer so you really want to contribute. There is a way to find out if the foundation is legit. Call the Better Business Bureau or better yet, check out their website, which lists numerous charity groups and whether or not they are approved. If you don't have access to the Internet, you can look them up in the blue section of the white pages under "Federal Agencies" or call information. They have tons of information on these places and they can let you know where your money will *really* go.

Be willing to donate your time as well as your money!

TIPS for Spending and Sharing

1) **Familiarize yourself** with the average price of the products you buy most often. This way you know what prices are too high. You can do this simply by browsing ads in the paper occasionally or checking prices while you're out shopping.

2) **Be aware** of special offers and discounts. For example, go to the movies early to get the matinee price.

3) **Wait.** If you don't need something right away, wait for it to go on sale before you buy it.

4) **Make a list** of the things you need before you go shopping and stick to it. This will help eliminate frivolous spending.

5) **Take advantage of sales.** Don't be afraid to spend a lot of money at one time if it will save you money in the future. For example, let's say your favorite hair conditioner is on sale for fifty cents. For a price like that, buy as much as you can. It's something you will always use, and buying it now will save you a lot of the money you would have eventually had to spend to buy it in the future. Another example would be if a store is going out of business in July and you bought $100 in presents for Christmas. It's worth sacrificing $100 at the moment so that you can save the extra money at Christmas time or use it to buy even more Christmas presents.

6) **Use coupons.**

7) Buy in bulk. The more things you buy at once, the cheaper each individual item will be. For example, if you go through a lot of pencils at school, buy a large box of them. You know you'll use them and it will save you money. Try shopping at warehouse clubs, where things are sold in large quantities and at cheaper prices.

8) Try generic brands. They often are just as good as the name brands, and most people can't even tell the difference.

9) Buy out of season. For example, right after Christmas there are huge sales to get all of the seasonal items out of stock. Buy things you know you can use for next year, like wrapping paper, cards, etc. It will save you a lot of money in the long run. You can also buy school clothes right before summer, when the stores are trying to clear them out. They'll be a lot cheaper.

10) Overlook the merchandise carefully before buying it and always think twice if it's a final sale. If something seems too cheap, it probably is. Check to see if something is wrong with the product. If it is a final sale, be doubly cautious because if there is something wrong with the product, there is nothing you can do about it once it's bought.

11) Check the receipt. Always double check your receipt to make sure you were not over-charged for anything or charged for something you didn't get at all.

12) Watch the price display. If you ever buy something at a store on sale, watch the price display when it is rung up to make sure you got the sale price. Also watch it to make sure things are not rung up more than once.

13) Don't be too shy to say if you think there was a mistake. If you think you were over-charged or there was a mistake, don't be afraid to say so. Just be polite and I'm sure the cashier will understand.

14) Start a gift fund. Try putting a portion of the money you save from smart spending into a bank or container and use it for charitable gifts. Think of something that is important to you and plan to give the money to help that cause.

Additional Resources

Books

Consumer Buying Guide
$6.99

The Better Business Bureau's Guide to Wise Buying
$7.95

Smart Questions for Savvy Shoppers
By: Dorothy Leeds
$8.99

Websites

http://www.bbb.org   (website for the Better Business Bureau)

PREPARING FOR THE FUTURE

Samantha's Sad Day

"It's really been getting cold early this year."

"Yeah, this weather is crummy. I don't even have a winter coat yet."

"What happened to that brown one you had?"

"The zipper broke. It was getting pretty old anyway."

"Well, you better get one soon. It's supposed to snow tomorrow."

"You're right. What time is it?"

"Four-thirty. Why?"

"We still got time to make it to the bank. You want to come and help me pick out a new coat?"

"Sure, Sam. I'm always up for shopping."

Samantha and Melanie went to the bank to get the money for the coat. Samantha wasn't sure how much her new coat would cost so she took out $200, which she hoped would be more than enough. Then they drove to the mall to hunt down a new winter coat.

"What kind of coat are you thinking of getting, Sam?"

"I think I want like a black leather one, something that won't fall apart like my other one. Like this one," Samantha said holding up a short black leather style.

"How much is it?" Melanie asked.

"Hmm...$199. I only took out two hundred from the bank, but I think I had some other money from yesterday. I wonder if I'll have enough for the tax," Samantha said reaching for her purse. "My purse!! I lost my purse!! I must have set it down when we were looking at the shoe store."

The two girls ran to the shoe store and Samantha's purse was just where she had left it, but when she opened it up all of her money was gone.

Chapter Nine
Opening a Checking Account

What happened to Samantha was not a good experience, but one thing that would have prevented that from happening (besides not setting her purse down) is having a checking account. If she had a checking account she wouldn't have had to try to guess how much the coat might cost or carry around that much cash that could be lost or stolen. These are just a couple of reasons why checking accounts are convenient.

Opening a checking account might not be something that you want to do until you're eighteen, but you should know how to do it when the time comes. Opening a checking account is about the same as opening a savings account. You can follow the same steps as you did in Chapter Seven. You should note when comparing different fees that many places offer totally free checking if you maintain a minimum balance or have your paychecks directly deposited. Check with your employer about direct deposit.

You probably should open your checking account at the same place where your savings are. This will allow for the easy transfer of funds between your saving account and your checking account. Most banks have a special number you can call, and by punching in a couple of codes you can take money from your savings account and put it into your checking account, or vice versa, and save yourself a trip to the bank. Many banks also provide this service through their website. This can be very useful. For example, if you went to the store and wrote a check for fifty dollars and then realized when you got home that you only had forty-five dollars in your checking account, you could go online and move five dollars from your savings account into your checking account. Check with your bank. Most will have pamphlets on display containing information about their website and telephone services.

If you decide to open a checking account at the same place that your savings account is at, many banks have pamphlets that you can fill out and mail so that you don't even have to go to the bank to open the account. On the next page is an example. It's very simple to fill out. As you can see, you simply need to give them the basic information about your identification and where you live, what you want written on your checks, and how much money you want to open the account with. You can give them your savings account number and request to withdraw a certain amount of money from your savings account to open your checking account. This way you don't even have to go to the bank.

With an Interest Checking Account you can still earn interest on your money, but it will be slightly less than what you would earn in a regular savings account. Typically the interest rate for checking accounts is 2% or less. There are other fees that you need to be aware of though. For example, bouncing a check can cost $15 or more. To bounce a check means to write a check when you don't have enough money in your account to pay for it. The bank will charge you a fee and often times the store you bounced the check at will also charge you. So this is definitely one thing you do not want to do. Checking accounts also usually have a fall-below fee, as was discussed in Chapter Seven, meaning you are charged for not having the required amount of money in your account. Some banks charge a monthly and/or per-check fee, so try to avoid these.

YES, I Want to Close the Book on High Fees! Please open my Interest Checking Account.

Credit Union Account Number _____

Date _____

Print or type ONLY the information you want imprinted on checks

Name (1) _____

Name (2) _____
                    (Must be joint owner)

Address _____

City _____

State _____ Zip _____

Indicate additional information you want printed on checks such as Social Security Number, Drivers License Number or Telephone Number.

_____

_____

_____

_____

Deposit Instructions

❏ I have enclosed a check or money order for
$ _____ to open my Interest Checking
Account. (Minimum opening deposit: $20)

❏ Please transfer $ _____ from my Regular
Savings Account to open my new Interest Checking
Account. (Minimum opening transfer: $20)

Once you open your checking account you can make deposits and withdrawals just as you did with your savings account, only you would fill out deposit and withdrawal slips specifically for your checking account. You also will need to know how to write a check. Fill out the example check using the instructions below. (Note that you should always write checks in pen so that no one can erase or change what you wrote.)

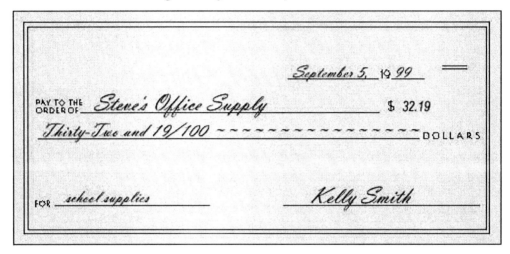

Steps for Writing a Check

1. Write the date in the area provided in the top right corner.

2. Write the name of the place or person for whom the check is for next to where it says, "Pay to the Order Of."

3. Write the amount of the check in numbers in the area provided next to the dollar sign.

4. Write out the amount in words on the line that ends with "DOLLARS." (You can write the change amount as a fraction of one hundred. ex. 04/100 would represent four cents)

5. Draw a wavy line from the end of the amount in words to where it says "Dollars." (This way no one can tamper or add to the amount you wrote.)

6. Write the purpose or what the check was for on the line in the lower left corner. (This is optional.)

7. Sign the line in the lower right corner with your official signature. Sign your name the same way every time.

Example: Complete the following check using the instructions and the example on the previous page.

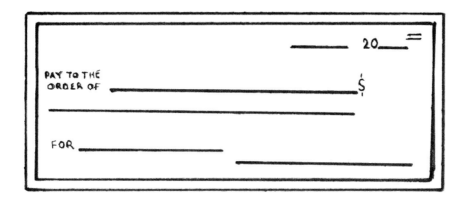

Every time you write a check, you should record it. You should also record any deposits that you make. Most checkbooks include a register, where you can keep track of all of the checks you write. Below is an example. Notice that you should write the check number, date, place or person to which the check was written, amount of the check, and the remaining balance in your checking account.

NUMBER	DATE	CODE	DESCRIPTION OF TRANSACTION	PAYMENT/DEBIT (-)	FEE (-)	TAX	DEPOSIT/CREDIT (+)	$ 318.72
1095	7/20		Steve's Office Supply	$ 32.19			$	286.53
	7/25		Deposit				42.95	329.48
	7/31		Deposit				59.62	389.10
1096	8/3		Kim Smith	65.50				323.60
	8/8		Deposit				58.75	382.35
	8/15		Deposit				47.88	430.23
	8/22		Deposit				59.62	489.85
	8/30		Withdrawal	20.00				469.85
	9/7		Deposit				49.48	519.33
1097	9/10		Kim Smith	65.50				453.83

When you receive your bank statement in the mail you can use your records to check the bank's records. Sometimes, however, your bank statement may not have all of the checks you have written or deposits you have made on it. This is because sometimes it takes checks a few days or more to get through the cycle, which may not have occurred by the time your bank statement was processed. Below are some steps you can use to reconcile, or check, if your records match the bank's.

How to Reconcile Your Bank Statement with Your Checkbook

1. Make sure that all of the checks listed on the statement are recorded in your checkbook. If not, and you know that you did write the check(s), record them in your checkbook and calculate the new balance.
2. Write the check number, date, and the amount of the checks that have not yet been deducted from your checking account (the ones that are not listed on the statement).

#	Date	Amount
___	___	___
___	___	___
___	___	___
___	___	___
	Total:	___

Add up all of the above checks and then subtract the total from the balance recorded on your bank statement. (Do all of your figuring on a separate sheet of paper. Do not write anything in your checkbook.)

3. If you made any deposits that are not listed on the bank statement, list them below.

Date	Amount
_____	_____
_____	_____
_____	_____
_____	_____
Total:	_____

Add this total to the balance on your bank statement.

4. The bank's total should now be equal to your total. If not, check for errors in your checkbook and on the statement. If you think the bank has made an error, call them and then write a letter explaining your dispute. The bank then has 45 days to resolve the discrepancy.

Note: This is also true with discrepancies involving your savings account.

To recap, essentially you start with your bank statement balance, subtract all checks that have not cleared and add deposits that were not processed before the statement's end date. You want your final number to reflect your true account balance after all the outstanding transactions go through.

For example, suppose you were given a checking account with $1000 in it and you were told that you must spend at least $500 of it. You only have four checks, so you can only spend it in four places. Write out the checks on the following pages to the places where you would choose to spend them and make up a fictional amount that you would spend.

_____ 20____ =

PAY TO THE
ORDER OF _____ $

_____

FOR _____

_____

_____ 20____ =

PAY TO THE
ORDER OF _____ $

_____

FOR _____

_____

TIPS for Using Your Checking Account

1) **Don't get a checking account until you need one and you know you're ready for it.**

2) **Don't use checks unless you have to.** Always pay cash if you can.

3) **Use your checks like you would cash.** Don't buy anything you wouldn't buy with cash out of your pocket.

4) **Don't write a check for something unless you know you have enough money in the bank to back it up.**

5) **Keep the required amount in your checking account to avoid the fall below fee.**

6) **Don't keep too much money in your checking account.** You'll make more interest in the regular savings and it will help prevent you from spending your savings. I recommend leaving $300 in it at all times and transferring more money over when you need it.

7) **<u>Always</u> record your purchases** made by check in your register.

8) **Sign your name the exact same way** each time.

Credit in Your World

Billy slumped down in his chair, his stomach growling. He looked around the roaring lunchroom where everyone was eating and laughing. He was doing neither. It was all because of a really stupid mistake he made two weeks ago…

"Hey, Tim, I forgot my lunch money today. You think you can lend me a couple bucks. I'll pay you back tomorrow."

"Yeah, no problem."

And with that Billy ate his lunch happily. The next day though, Tim wanted his money back.

"Oh, I'll bring it tomorrow, Tim. I promise. I was just late getting up this morning, and, being in such a hurry, I totally forgot."

"Okay, bring it tomorrow then."

But the next day, Billy didn't bring Tim's money, and he didn't bring it the day after that either. In fact, after a week had gone by, Tim got sick of asking for his money every day, so he decided he would never lend Billy money again.

Today, Billy forgot his lunch money again, but this time no one would lend him any money. After everyone at the lunch table saw how Billy neglected to pay Tim back, they didn't want to wind up in the same situation. They knew that if they "lent" Billy the money they would never see it again.

The reason the boys wouldn't lend Billy the money was because he had created a bad credit rating for himself, whether he realized it or not. Credit is trust in a person's ability and intention to pay back borrowed money. For example, if I wanted to borrow $1,000,000 I probably wouldn't be able to get anyone to loan it to me because my yearly income does not give me the *ability* to pay it back. In Billy's case, he lost his credit because he lacked the *intention* of paying his loan. By not paying Tim back, Billy proved that he did not take keeping his promises seriously, and therefore the other boys could not trust him. Luckily for Billy, the only thing he was missing out on was his lunch, but in today's society bad credit can lead to a lot bigger problems than that. Let's take a look at Karen and Bob.

Karen and Bob are married and are living in Karen's mother's house, who has just recently passed away. Because there were four children, Karen is given one fourth of the house and must buy back the other three fourths from her brothers. She is not used to paying a house payment every month, so she and her husband have a new system of spending to adapt to. Unfortunately, however, they do not want to change their spending habits and continue splurging on fast food and Bingo every week, thinking that they are going to win the money to pay the house payment. Things somehow don't work out that way and at the end of the month they have to scrounge up the money to pay the bill. After about five months they just can't handle it anymore, and soon they have bills piling up that they just can't pay. They start using credit cards to pay off other credit cards until they are in an endless cycle of debt. Finally, they declare bankruptcy and their bills are cleared, but now their credit rating is scarred for the next ten years.

Somehow, they still don't learn the importance of credit and continue their frivolous spending. Bills are late, and their credit rating sinks even lower. Then, it happens. The inevitability that their car wouldn't last forever finally comes to life, and it is time to buy a new car, or at least a new, used car. Of course Karen and Bob can't afford to pay cash for a car, not many people can, but who will lend them money now, knowing that they don't have much ability or intention of paying it back? Companies who take advantage of high risk debtors by charging them astronomical interest rates will. Hey, high risks are met with high rates.

Now, Karen and Bob are paying $469 a month for a used car, which they will be paying for the next five years, when they could have bought a new car for that very same amount. Karen and Bob try as hard as they can to make the payments on the car and the house every month, but it is very difficult and they are just barely making it. Then, one day the car's brakes stop functioning properly. It is definitely not safe to drive a car without reliable brakes, so they take it to get fixed. It will cost $500, but they don't have any money saved and they don't have credit. This is an emergency situation where credit is a lifesaver. If Karen and Bob had a good credit rating they could simply charge it and have at least a month to come up with only the minimum payment, but Karen and Bob don't have good credit and now they're in a jam. Without the money, they can't get their car fixed, they won't be able to get to work, they won't be able to pay their bills, and they'll be stuck in the cycle of debt once again. They can't let that happen, so they sell a couple of items and come up with the $500. With the money they spent on the car repairs they have a hard time paying the bill at the end of the month and get behind on their payments. Once they get behind it is very hard for them to get back on track again and before you know it, they get a letter in the mail threatening the repossession of their car - yes, the used one they're paying way too much for.

Hopefully, most people won't find themselves in a situation as bad as that, but it is true that bad credit can cause all of those problems. All of that can be avoided, though, through just a few simple steps. First, of all one must be organized and have his or her own method of keeping track of ALL important financial documents. The person has to know his or her monthly income, monthly expenditures, and from that develop a budget. A person should not make purchases he or she cannot afford. By "afford" I do not mean that one should be able to pay cash for all of his or her purchases, but to make decisions based on how much he or she can afford to pay monthly.

Clearly, most people cannot afford to pay cash for a house, but many can afford to be loaned the money, using their credit, to pay it back over a period of time, month by month.

Credit does not only lead to situations like Karen and Bob's. That's only where bad credit will lead you. Good credit will take you to many beautiful places. It can lead you in your new car, from your own home, to the mall where you can "buy now and pay later." And as you saw with Karen and Bob it can actually save you money, considering the high interest rates that face those who are high risks to loaning institutions.

Sidney Bernstein is a great example of the use of good credit. He has always paid his bills and worked hard. He wanted to open his own business, a Jewish styled deli. He certainly did not have the money to start the business on his own, so he needed someone to have faith in his ideas and loan him the money.

Loaning institutions look at many factors when considering granting a person a loan, especially a large loan, such as the one Sidney would need to open his restaurant. They don't just consider how much money you make. They look at where you work, how long you've been there, what you do, how long you have lived in your current residency, your age, your marital status, etc. There are numerous things they review in order to determine your credit, character, capacity, and commitment. Sidney's credit rating looked good and his business plan sounded like a good risk, so they gave him the loan. Nine years later, Sidney has everything he's ever wanted in life. He has a successful business, a new truck, a new boat, and a house he loves, all thanks to good credit.

Credit ratings affect *everyone*. Just how it will affect you all depends on how you use it. If it is used carelessly, like in Karen and Bob's case, it can lead to disastrous results, but if used wisely, like in Sidney's case, it can have glorious results. To get the glorious results it only takes a few quick steps: be organized, know your financial situation, and be responsible. The choice is yours.

Chapter Ten
Obtaining Good Credit

The scenarios that you just read about should have given you a pretty good idea about how credit can work for, or against, you. Following this chapter are some major tips that can help make it work for you, but there are some other things you should know about, too.

First of all, there are three major credit bureaus that keep track of everyone's credit history, as well as a limited amount of personal history, such as your name, address, place of employment, etc. They know who's been paying their bills and who hasn't. They know if you pay your bills on time or if you've been late once or twice. When a person wants a loan or applies for a credit card, the issuers of these things can contact one of the credit bureaus and get a report on you. It can make or break your chances of getting the loan or the credit card. And guess what. Even prospective employers can run a credit check on you before they decide if they want to hire you or not, so your credit rating can affect whether you'll get a loan for a new house or if you'll get that job you applied for.

The good news is that you probably don't have a credit rating yet, which means you are in full control of determining what it will be. You can plan ahead so that when you do get a credit rating, it will be a good one. You can start creating a good credit rating by applying for a credit card when you're eighteen. Charge a couple of things, and then pay the bill in full at the end of the month. Only good things will happen if you do that. If you at least pay the minimum payment, which is the minimum amount that the credit card company is requiring you to pay, it will not hurt your credit rating, but it may hurt your pocket book.

Credit card companies like to make money, so they really like it when you only pay the minimum payment because then you have to pay them interest on the remaining balance. Credit card companies can charge as high as 20%, or more, interest per year on the amount you owe them. For this reason you should always pay the bill off in full, if possible, but also try to find a low rate credit card in case you do wind up paying interest. You should also try to avoid cards that charge annual fees, unless you expect to carry a balance and it offers a lower rate than other cards without annual fees.

The good thing about credit cards is that once you charge something you have a grace period in which you do not have to pay for it. This is usually about 25-30 days. So you can buy something you need now, but pay for it a month later. If, however, you're not sure if the money to pay the bill will be there at the end of the month, don't charge it.

If you lose your credit card, call the company and cancel it right away. It's a good precaution to keep a list of all of your credit cards, their limits, their expiration dates, and their numbers in a safe place at home so that you can give that information to the company if the card is stolen or lost. If the card is stolen and someone charges $1000 on it, don't worry. The maximum amount you will have to pay is $50, no matter how much they charge on your card. Nevertheless, don't waste any time in canceling the card. No matter how you slice it, someone is getting ripped off for *every* penny that thief charges, even if you're not the one to pay for it.

If you use your credit cards wisely and pay your bills on time (credit bills as well as others), you should develop a good credit rating, but it's a good idea to check your credit report annually. There could be an error, and you don't want to be held accountable for something you didn't do. Each person is entitled to one free credit report per year. To receive one, send your name, addresses from up to five years, social security number, date of birth, and a copy of your driver's license to one of the credit bureaus. Each of their addresses are listed at the end of this chapter under "Additional Resources."

Credit is really very simple. Be sensible, be punctual, and follow the tips at the end of this chapter and you should only see the good side of credit.

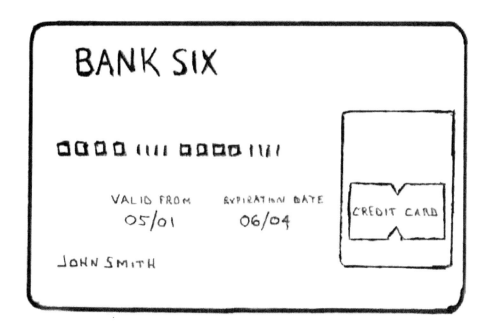

TIPS for Using Your Credit Card

1) **Don't mistake your credit card for free money.** The bill will come at the end of the month and you will have to pay for your purchases.

2) **Pay cash if you can.** Don't charge anything unless you need to.

3) **If the bill will be around longer than the product, don't buy it.** Imagine how discouraging it would be to be paying for something you no longer had.

4) **Don't use your credit card to buy perishables**, such as food, or to pay for leisure activities. If you don't have the cash for these things, you shouldn't spend it. (This also fits the test in Tip #3. The food would be long gone by the time you pay the bill.)

5) **Know your credit card limit and your own financial limits.** Keep track of how much you charge so you don't go over them. You also want to keep track so that you don't get charged for anything you didn't spend. (You can use an extra check register to keep track or use one of the forms provided at the end of this book.)

6) **Only get one to two credit cards.** The more you have the more you'll be likely to spend, the more problems you'll have if your purse or wallet gets stolen, and the lower your chances will be of getting a loan. When you apply for a loan, the bank assumes that you could charge up every one of those cards to the limit if you wanted to, and if you did that, then your chances of paying back the loan would not be as good.

7) Always pay the bill in full or the maximum amount you possibly can.

There's no sense giving money away to credit card companies when there are much better things you could be doing with it.

Additional Resources

Books

What Everyone Should Know About Credit Before Buying or Borrowing Again
By: Ira U. Cobleigh and the editors of U.S. News & World Report Books

Three Main Credit Bureaus

Experian
Box 2002
Allen, TX 75013
1-888-397-3742
http://www.experian.com

Equifax Credit Information Services
Box 740241
Atlanta, GA 30374
1-800-685-1111
http://www.equifax.com

Trans Union Corporation
Box 7000
North Olmsted, OH 44070
1-800-888-4213
http://www.tuc.com

Websites

http://loan.yahoo.com/c

http://www.equifax.com/personal_solutions/index.html.

http://www.yourcredit.com

http://www.creditinfocenter.com

A Typical Day

"Oh no! I'm running late again." David threw on his hat and booked out the door.

"Man, I'm glad it's only a five minute drive to school," David thought. "I think I'm going to make it."

David glided into his first hour class just before the bell.

*   *   *

"Hey, David. You mind if I hitch a ride with you to math today? My car's in the shop."

"Sure, Mark. No problem."

David and Mark were taking a math class at the community college as a part of their high school schedule.

*   *   *

"Thanks for the ride David. So what are you planning on doin' today?"

"Well, I got do a lot of running. I got to go up to the pizzeria to pick up my paycheck, run to the bank, get some gas, go to the store for my mom, and then I'm going to stop by Lynn's."

"Well, hey if you're done by about seven, meet us up at Burger Billy's. You can bring Lynn, too, if you want."

"Alright. I'll probably see you later then, Mark."

Chapter Eleven
Buying a Used Car

If your schedule is anything like David's, you'll probably need to have a car pretty soon. Just think of how great that would be. You could drive yourself to school, to work, and to a friend's house without having to worry about when your parents' car is available. Sometimes having a car is not only convenient, it's a necessity. If Joe's parents didn't have an extra car and they had to drive him everywhere, think of how many trips they would have to make each day. They would have to drop him off at school, pick him up from the high school, take him to the community college for his math class, pick him up from there an hour later, take him to work, and also go without a car some afternoons to let him go out with it. Many parents would rather give their kid a car than go through all that, and many will, but if you're not in that category it's time to start thinking about how *you* can get a car.

If you know you're going to need a car, you need to figure out how much you can afford. Don't even start looking until you know your price range. You may find yourself getting too attached to things you can't have. To figure out how much you can afford fill in the worksheet on the next page.

What I Can Afford (for buying a car)

Savings (money that you currently have saved in your bank account)

_____

Bonds (money that you have saved in bonds)

_____

Available Money (any other money that you currently have access to)

_____

Gifts (Ask your parents if they are willing to give you any of the money for your car, and write the amount of their offer on the line.)

_____

Loan (Ask your parents if they are willing to loan you some of the money, and write the amount of their offer.)   _____

Total: _____

This is the amount of money you currently have access to, but don't plan on spending every dime of it. Leave at least $500 out for an unexpected car repair. Buying a used car can be risky and you don't want to take any chances.

Minus $500 for Possible Car Repairs   _____-$500_____

New Total: _____

This is the **maximum** amount you can afford to spend on the car itself, but once you buy the car there will be more expenses such as gas, maintenance, and car insurance. Most states have laws requiring a minimum amount of insurance, so you must consider these ongoing costs of the car. Use the chart below to figure out exactly how much you can afford monthly.

What I Can Afford (for monthly car expenses)

Monthly Income (how much you make each month)

_____

Minus **Average Monthly Expenses** (refer back to your expenditure charts in Chapter Six)   -   _____

Total: _____

(This is the amount you have left to work with, after your regular expenses, to pay for gas, insurance, and maintenance. The amount each person spends on gas per month will vary and will change as prices do.

Total (from above):   _____

Minus **Monthly Cost of Gas**   -   _____

New Total: _____

This is the amount you can afford for the remaining car expenses, such as repairs and insurance. You want to be prepared for these expenses, so if it doesn't seem like you'll have enough money to make it, you may need to revise your budget, cut down on frivolous spending, and maybe even start working a few more hours per week. If you can't afford to work any more, maybe your parents would split the insurance bill with you. Many parents understand the difficulty of keeping up with these bills while concentrating on school, so they'll probably be willing to help you out. If you think that you can do it on your own, however, DO IT! Don't take advantage of your parents just because you can. Anything that you can afford to pay for yourself you should. Your parents have bills, too.

Deciding What Kind of Car You Want

The next big step is to pick about three car models that you think would suit you and your budget. You already know the maximum amount you can spend, so that may rule out your dream car. Now is the time to be realistic. Answer the following questions below to help decide what kind of car would work best for you.

1. What would I be using the car for most often? (can be more than one thing)

_____

_____

_____

_____

2. How much room would *I* need?

_____

3. Would I be driving long distances or short distances most commonly?

_____

4. Do I want a car or a truck?

_____

If you would be using the car to drive yourself and your friends to hockey practice and lug all of your equipment you would probably need a medium to large car. If you normally are only driving yourself and your book bag, then maybe a smaller car, or even a truck, would be convenient. Trucks are a nice option for teenagers because if you're one of the first of your friends to get a car, you could get trapped into becoming a taxi service, only *you'll* be paying all the bills. If you can only fit two people in your truck, you may not find yourself in that situation as often. If you would be driving long distances, you definitely want a car that's reliable. Of course no matter where you'd be driving you would want your car to be reliable.

Go to the library to research specific car models and their reliability. You want to do a lot of research and talking to friends and family about the car models you are interested in. If your aunt has a car model she has found to be particularly reliable, perhaps you may want to consider it. After you have researched it and thought it over, write down two or three car models that you seriously plan on buying. It is easier to comparison shop for two or three cars than just browsing the lot for anything.

Car Models I Would Like to Buy

1._____

2._____

3._____

You know your price range and you have a good idea of what kind of car you want, but there are a few other questions you should ask yourself before you begin looking. Answer the questions below so that you know what you expect from the car you're going to buy.

What Do I Expect of the Car I Buy

1. Do I want an automatic or manual transmission?_____

2. Do I need air conditioning?_____

3. Do I want a two-door or a four-door?_____

4. Do I need a radio? CD Player?_____

5. Do I want power locks, windows, and seat belts?_____

6. List anything else you definitely want your car to have on the following lines.

_____

_____

_____

_____

_____

_____

_____

_____

Now that you know your price limit, what models you are looking for, and what options you would like to have, you're ready to do some shopping. Buying a used car can be scary, especially if you don't know the person you're buying it from. That's why you should always try to buy from people you know first. When buying a used car, you can't trust anyone more than your parents. Talk to them about possibly buying one of their old cars. Perhaps they'd like to get a new car anyway, and sell you the old one. That way you would know the car you're buying and you would know its condition. Plus, your parents would probably give you a good price. If, however, your parents can't afford this or don't go with this plan you'll have to start looking elsewhere for a car.

Besides your parents, check with other friends and relatives to see if they know anyone selling a used car. Why a used car? If you can afford a new car, by all means consider buying one, but most teenagers can't afford that so buying a used car is the only option. A new car instantly goes down in value the second you drive it off the lot, usually by thousands of dollars! Since cars depreciate in value (become worth less and less over time), buying a used car allows you to buy cheap so there's less to lose. If you can squeeze 5 years out of a $4,000 used car, you will make out better economically than if you only get 10 years out of a $15,000 new car. (Of course this is assuming that the amount of money spent on repairs between the two cars was equal.) As this example demonstrates, you could buy two $4,000 used cars in 10 years, for a total of $8,000, or spend $15,000 (almost twice as much) for a new car that lasted the same amount of time. This is not to discourage against buying a new car, because they can be more reliable and provide better accommodations, but at an age where money is scarce a used car should serve your purpose until you can afford more. Also remember that a new car would cost you more for insurance than a used one.

If you can't find anyone you know selling a car, then start looking elsewhere. You can check in local publications which specialize in classified ads. Often these publications are filled with ads from people trying to sell everything from computers to cars. Each ad lists the person's name and number, and you simply call if you are interested. You also should keep your eyes peeled while passing through the neighborhood. Maybe the person around the block has a "For Sale" sign on his car. Take a look. Sometimes people park their cars on empty lots with "For Sale" signs on them, so others, who may be interested, can stop and look at them. Used cars are everywhere. You can also buy from a used car dealership, but be careful. You never know what you're going to get. If you do go to a dealership, be sure to bring someone older and more knowledgeable, either a parent, friend, or relative. If you know any mechanics bring them along for sure. For the average person, however, there are some simple things to look for. On the next page are some tips that will show you some signs to beware of.

TIPS for Buying a Used Car

1) **Avoid used luxury cars.** They're expensive to repair and the insurance is high.

2) **Don't buy anything bigger than what you'll need.**

3) **If the car isn't even clean, the owner could be trying to hide scratches or a bad paint finish.**

4) **Check to make sure the color of paint matches throughout the car.** Mismatched paint may mean the car has been in an accident.

5) **Open and close the car door to test it.**

6) **A dealership will probably charge the highest prices for a used car.**

7) **Never smile.** It will make you look too eager to buy.

8) **Never chew gum.** It will make you look like you know less than you do.

9) **Bring a mirror and use it to look underneath the car.** Check for rusting and leaks.

10) **If it's raining** when you look at the car, it would be difficult to see cracks in the windshield. **Look at the car again when it's dry out.**

11) **Check to see if all four tires are the same.**

12) Open the hood and look for anything that looks like a bad sign, rust, etc. Just opening the hood shows that you're not going to buy any piece of junk.

13) Testdrive the car and all of its accessories: radio, lights, heat, air conditioning, turn signal, windshield wipers, windows, locks, etc. Test everything you can think of.

Additional Resources

Books

The Used Car Buyer's Manual
By: David J. Buechel
$9.95

Free Information

"Nine Ways to Lower Your Auto Insurance"
Insurance Information Institute
110 William Street
New York, NY 10038
212-669-9250

"How to Keep Your Car from Being Stolen"
1-800-23-SHELL

Lucy's Exciting Day

"Hey, Lucy, there's a big envelope here for you. It's from the university and it says "First Class." It looks like it could be good news."

"It must be my reply from my scholarship application," Lucy was excited.

"Oh, the scholarship application you blamed me for losing when it was in *your* bag?" her mom teased.

Lucy looked down, "Sorry, Mom. You do have a tendency to misplace things, though."

"Do you think I got the scholarship?"

"Well, I don't know why they'd need to send you a rejection letter in a big manila envelope. Go ahead and open it."

"My whole future sits in this envelope. This determines how much I'll have to pay for college and if I'll have to plan on working more hours," Lucy babbled.

"Oh, come on and open it. I'm getting excited here!" her mom urged.

"Okay, okay," Lucy began to open the envelope slowly. "Congratulations on being selected as a full tuition scholarship recipient," she read. "I got it! I got it!" she screamed.

"I knew you could do it!" her mom joined in.

What an exciting day!

Chapter Twelve
Getting Money for College

If you would like to go to college, don't let any money problems stop you. There are so many ways to get free money and/or loans that you should never let money come between you and your goal. The first source of aid you should look for is scholarship money because it does not have to be repaid. When you are granted a scholarship, usually the check goes straight to your college where you can use it toward your tuition and other fees. The money never has to be paid back. There are many places you can look for these scholarships. Below are some examples.

Where to Find Scholarships

1. **The counselor's office** - Ask your counselor for a list of available scholarships.

2. **The university you plan to attend** - You could be eligible for scholarships straight from the university you plan to attend. Ask your counselor if she knows of any or call the university directly.

3. **The Federal Government** - Apply for financial aid from the government. Ask your counselor for a F.A.F.S.A., Free Application for Federal Student Aid, form which may also make you eligible for state aid. (You can also get this form at your local library.)

4. **The Internet** - Check this web site
   http://www.finaid.org and use search engines to find others.

5. **The Library** - There are many books that are filled with scholarship opportunities. Check at the end of this chapter under "Additional Resources" for specific titles of these books.

6. **Department Stores** - Stores like Target and J.C. Penney often offer scholarships to students.

7. **Financial Institutions** - Some banks and credit unions offer scholarships to the children of their members.

8. **Private organizations** - Many organizations offer assistance to students who may become an asset to them in the future. For example, the Society of Women Engineers offers scholarships to assist female students going into engineering.

9. **DON'T use scholarship searches that cost money.** You may be mailed something that offers you a scholarship search for a price. Don't do it. You can find most of the same scholarship offers in the places listed above, so why pay them for something you can do yourself.

The best place to look is your counselor's office. Many private organizations, universities, companies, department stores, etc. send their scholarship application forms directly to the counselors so that they can make them available to the students. The federal aid forms can also usually be found in your counselor's office. Don't just limit yourself to your counselor's office. Keep your eyes peeled for scholarship opportunities everywhere you go.

Once you have found some appealing scholarship opportunities, it's time to get them. Most scholarships have requirements. Some are looking for academic distinction. Others are looking for athletic distinction. Some just want a person who puts a lot into their school and their community. No matter who you are or what you're good at, there will be something out there for you.

Before you even begin to fill out the application, there are some things you can do to make yourself a more likely candidate.

Before the application

1. **Pull your grades up.** More than anything else, your grades are the most important thing on your scholarship application. There will always be opportunities for everyone, even with a low grade point average, but many scholarship applications require at least a 3.0 G.P.A., or a B average. So try to work up to that, or if you're already above that keep it up. Don't stop at any limit, just do the <u>best</u> you can. On the "Additional Resources" page at the end of this chapter are some books you can use to help you.

2. **Improve you're A.C.T. and S.A.T. scores.** Many universities use a quick formula to determine who will be eligible for their academic scholarships. An example of one of these formulas is to recalculate the grade point average including only academic courses (no electives), multiplying it by ten, and then adding the A.C.T. score. My theory is that they then take the top scores for as many scholarships that they plan to give out. I suspect that they determine from there who gets a partial scholarship and who gets a full by comparing extracurricular activities. I believe this because the people who make it into the "pot" are all very intelligent and some grade points may be higher simply because of more availability of A.P. and college courses or not as rigorous of courses, in which good grades would come more easily. Though different universities may use different formulas, you usually will need the grades

and test scores to become eligible for money and then you can use your extracurricular activities to get more. (Look under "Additional Resources" for books to help you bring up your test scores.)

3. **Join a club.** Start joining clubs, as many as you can. Do it because you care about the purpose and your school, but guaranteed they'll help you gain scholarship money. People don't want to give money to lazy bums who sit and watch TV all day. Being involved at school now shows that you will probably get involved in college and make a difference there. When colleges offer scholarships, they hope that their recipients will do something special one day and say that they attended that university. Nothing is a better advertisement than when the man who invented the computer says, "I learned everything I know at Blank University." If you don't do much now how can they expect some great accomplishment from you in the future.

4. **Join a sport.** Colleges and scholarship judges like well-rounded individuals. They like to see people who are intelligent, involved, and physically fit. They don't know if you're fit unless you're on a sport.

5. **Try something new.** To be well rounded you have to try new and different things. Keep your mind open to new ideas. Pick up an instrument, try out for the school play, or sing in the choir. Choose something that you think you would really enjoy.

6. **Run for class president.** Any leadership position you can get your hands on will look great on a scholarship application. It shows that you are outgoing, well liked, and a leader, which are all things that they are looking for.

7. **Become active in your community.** Volunteer for a walk-a-thon or a bake sale. Do something for a cause you care about. You'll feel better about yourself, you'll be helping your community and a worthy cause, and

you will be increasing your chances for scholarships. It's a good idea all around.

8. **Get a job.** We already talked about the advantage of having a job listed on your college and scholarship applications. It will show that you are responsible and not afraid of hard work.

All of things mentioned above will increase your chances of gaining scholarship money, but you shouldn't do any of them for solely that reason. Do the things above because you really care about your school and community or because you simply enjoy it, but don't just try to join everything if you're not going to put your heart into it. There are a lot of things listed above, but please do not feel like you have to do all of them. You don't want to overdo it and drain yourself or sacrifice your grades. Just do as much as you can without feeling overwhelmed. Everyone has different talents, so try to expand on one of yours.

Examining the Application

Before you fill out the application, look at the requirements. What is it that they want you to have to apply for their scholarship? Now if you don't fit the requirements. . . Let's say it says you need to have a 3.5 grade point average to apply and you only have a 3.4 . . . don't let that stop you. You may have other qualities to make up for the difference. If you have a lot of applications to fill out, however, start with the ones that you fit all of the requirements for and have a better chance at. If you are really off on the requirements, though . . . Let's say you only have a 2.0 G.P.A. . . . you may not even want to bother.

There is another reason why you should carefully look at the requirements. The requirements give you a pretty good idea of what type of people they want to give their scholarships to. If you know that you exemplify the traits that they are looking for, be sure to emphasize those qualities. Look at the name of the scholarship. Some make it very obvious what they're looking for. For example, if it's called the All-Around Scholarship, they're looking for someone who is well rounded, involved in their school and the community and shows interest in many different things. If it includes the word "academic" in it anywhere you can be sure your grades and your test scores will play a big role. If it contains the word "athletic" you want to include all of your athletic experience. The point is to get an idea for what they're looking for so that you can emphasize those aspects of your life. You want to give them as many reasons as you can for choosing you.

Organizing Your Achievements

Once you start filling out a lot of applications, you'll realize that most of them want much of the same information. To make things easier on yourself and to help prevent forgetting some of your accomplishments, fill in the list on the next few pages, make a copy, and then use it when filling out each application, or make a similar list on your computer and keep it updated.

My Scholastic Record

High School: _____

High School Address: _____

_____

Cumulative GPA: _____

Class Rank: _____

A.C.T. Composite Score: _____

        English   _____

        Math   _____

        Reading   _____

        Science   _____

S.A.T. Composite Score: _____

        Verbal   _____

        Math   _____

Advance Placement/College Classes Taken: (Include scores if A.P. Exam was taken.)

_____

_____

_____

_____

_____

_____

_____

High School Activities:

_____

_____

_____

_____

_____

_____

Community and Volunteer Activities:

_____

_____

_____

_____

_____

_____

Work Experience: (Include name and address of places of employment)

Name: _____

Address: _____

_____

Name: _____

Address: _____

_____

Name: _____

Address: _____

_____

Awards and Honors:

_____

_____

_____

_____

_____

_____

_____

_____

_____

_____

Now it's time to fill out the application.

1. **Print in black ink or type it.** There are only two ways an application should ever be filled out - printed neatly in black ink or typed. First check what the application says. Many specify that they want it typed or that it must be in ink. Even if it doesn't say black ink, black is considered more professional so you should use it anyway.

2. **Be neat.** If you know your handwriting isn't very good - NEVER print by hand. Always type it. One of the worst things you can do is submit an application that is hardly legible. I wouldn't doubt that most sloppy applications wind up straight in the trash. Would you want to waste your time trying to read someone else's sloppy handwriting? Probably not, so don't waste your time filling out the application if it's not going to be neat. If you don't have a typewriter, borrow a friend's or use one at school.

3. **Make sure everything is filled out completely.** If you leave anything blank the person reviewing the scholarship may think you have something

to hide or they might not get all of the information they need to make a decision. Before you mail out each application, double check that every blank and requirement has been fulfilled.

4. **Don't rush to mail it out.** If the deadline is at least a month or two away, give it some time. You never know what other awards you may receive or extra achievements you will make in that time that you can use for your benefit. If the application asks for you're A.C.T. score or your grade point average and you think you might be able to bring it up before the deadline, wait until you receive your new scores, but don't wait too long. Try to mail everything within ten days of the due date or a week before the postmark date.

5. **Keep track of the deadlines and the items that must be included.** Make a list, like the one below, of every scholarship you plan to apply for and put the deadline next to each one. Below each one, list the things that must be included with the application. For example, an essay, recommendation, or high school transcript. Also include when you will be notified (if it says) and the date you mailed it out. Post this list somewhere that you can refer to it quickly. (At the back of this book there is a blank list you can use.)

List of Scholarships That I Have Applied For

1. Target All-Around Scholarship   Due: 11/1/01

   Include: completed application, one page list of volunteer activities, high school transcript, essay

   Notified by: 2/10/02

   Mailed: 10/15/01

2. Voice of Democracy   Due: 11/15/01

> Include: completed application, high school transcript, audio cassette of my spoken essay
>
> Notified by: 2/02
>
> Mailed: 11/1/01

3. University of Michigan-Dearborn Chancellor's Scholarship

> Due: 12/15/01
>
> Include: completed application, high school transcript, copy of A.C.T. score, essay, two letters of recommendation
>
> Notified by: 1/31/02
>
> Mailed: Not Yet

4. Michigan Society of Professional Engineers Scholarship   Due: 1/15/02

> Include: completed application, high school transcript, 250 word typed essay, copy of A.C.T. score
>
> Notified by: 4/02
>
> Mailed: Not yet

6. **Always include a copy of you're A.C.T. score when applying for a university scholarship.** If you took the A.C.T. more than once and have improved your score, this is very important. Many colleges might only have your first and lowest score on record, which means you wouldn't get credit for your new and improved score. Send them a copy just to make sure they know you've done better.

7. **Choose carefully whom you want to write your recommendations.** Many scholarship opportunities require you to obtain one or more letters of recommendation from teachers, counselors, or other people who know you well. Since most scholarships are geared to help you in getting a

college education, most want to know what type of student you are and if you have the ability to succeed. For this reason I recommend asking a teacher, counselor, sports coach, or club sponsor. Recommendations are very useful in determining what type of person you are and how other people think of you. With this in mind, you definitely want to pick someone who knows you well and thinks highly of you. Try to think of the area of school in which you are, or were, most involved. If you are an athlete, perhaps you would want a coach to write about your determination and perseverance. If you have been actively involved in a certain club, perhaps you could have the sponsor write about your school spirit and dedication. If you are an excellent student ask your favorite teacher for a recommendation. If you're not sure who to ask try to develop a relationship with a teacher or get involved in something so that a teacher can get to know you better.

8. **Get recommendations in advance.** Teachers and counselors are busy people so be sure that you give them enough time to prepare a good recommendation for you. If you give it to them the day before you need it, and they have ten million other things to do, they may not be thinking very highly of you when they write it.

9. **Make things easy on your counselor.** It is to your advantage to buy a pack of manila envelopes and address each scholarship application yourself. This way you know it will be going to the right place and it will save your counselor the time. Secondly, place a post-it note on the envelope with everything you need the counselor to do. For example if you need a high school transcript, write that. Sometimes scholarship applications require a counselor to briefly describe the grading system at your school or to fill in the required academic information. Also write the deadline in capital letters on the post-it note so your counselor will know exactly when to mail it out and it will get there in time. Whatever else you

can do yourself, do it. If it asks for copies of you're A.C.T. score, make them yourself. When you've gotten your part completed, put it all in the addressed envelope, with the post-it note on top, and give it to your counselor two weeks in advance, if possible.

10. **Save your money in your parents' name.** Currently the American Government expects you to be able to contribute 35% of your savings to your college education, but only about 5.6% of your parents'. Thus you will probably be more likely to receive federal funds if you keep the money in your parents' name.

Writing an Essay for a Scholarship

If the scholarship application asks for an essay, that essay is probably going to play a pretty important role in your possible selection. An essay, written by you, shows how you think and what type of person you are. The first thing to do is look at exactly what they are asking you. Don't go off on your own tangent. Give them the information they're looking for. Some just want to know a little bit about you. Some want to know about your goals or future plans. Make sure you're telling them what they want to know, not what you feel like writing about. Be honest about yourself, but emphasize your good points and the things that the scholarship application seems to focus on.

Your essay can also show whether or not you know how to spell or write coherently so that's where you have to be careful. Make sure that you write clearly and in complete sentences. Whatever you do, make sure there are no spelling errors in your essay. Have an English teacher, or two, read it and ask for their suggestions. (Note: I would recommend saving your essays on a computer or make copies of them. You may be able to use the same essay for three different scholarships.)

Once you've applied for all of the scholarships you can, all you can do is wait. I like to write next to each scholarship when I can expect to be notified if I am selected. That way, if I haven't heard anything by then I know that I can just assume that I didn't get it and cross it out. It makes me feel better to know the facts than to be left wondering.

Filling out scholarship applications is something everyone should do no matter where they are going or how much it costs, but if you don't expect to see too much scholarship money and you don't want to take out a hefty loan, there are ways to go to college for less. One way is to attend your local community college for the first two years and then transfer over to a university. You just have to be careful that you take classes that will transfer to the university you plan to attend. Going to a community college first will really save a lot of money because you can live at home, hence no room and board fees, and tuition itself is cheaper. In the meantime, you can try to save up more money to go to the university. If you still don't think you have enough for room and board after two years at community college, pick a public university that you can drive to. Going to school at a public university in your state is also a lot cheaper than going to one out of state. Obviously, when you are deciding on a university, you want to find some place that you will be comfortable and can make the most of your education, so keep this in mind as well as the price.

An important thing to remember is that college is what **you** make of it. If you want to learn, you will learn. If you don't want to take the time to study you will not learn as much. This is true no matter where you go. Just like anything else, you will only get out of it what you put into it. So don't feel like you have to go to the most expensive university to get a good job someday. Once you get your foot in the door, and usually a four-year college education can do that, your abilities will speak for themselves. Check out some of the books at the end of this chapter. They'll help you pick out a good, yet affordable, college.

Loans

If you know that between you, your parents, and your scholarships you're still going to need more money for college, by all means get a loan. Your college education is so important today that borrowing some money to get it is very worthwhile, and the extra money you'll make because of it more than makes up for it. Use the chart on the following page to determine how much you'll need and then review your options with your parents. Typically you should be able to obtain the best loans from the federal government and you should only resort to a loan from the bank after all other means have been utilized.

How Much Will I Need to Borrow for College

Total Cost of College

1. Yearly tuition   _____

2. Books (estimated)   _____

3. Room and Board (if necessary)   _____

4. Supplies (estimated)   _____

5. Registration/Parking/Other fees   _____

Total 1:   _____

Total Money Available

1. My Money Saved   _____

2. My Parents' Contribution/College Fund   _____

3. Other contributions (from friends and family)   _____

4. Scholarships   _____

Total 2:   _____

      Total 1   _____

      <u>**Minus Total 2**</u>   _____

             = Remaining Amount Needed   _____

TIPS for Getting Money for College

1) **Apply for as much as you can.** You never know what you might get.

2) **Enter contests.** For example, many places have essay contests and your essay, not your high school transcript, determines who wins. So if you have good writing skills, but not so good grades, this might be a good thing to give a shot.

3) **Don't overdo it and don't over-dramatize your accomplishments.** Don't say that your mission in life is to save the world and restore it to perfection. Corny things like that can get your application trashed.

4) **Don't be too wordy. Big words aren't necessarily better.** The more simple and readable your essay and application are, the better your chances are.

5) **Don't lie, exaggerate, or say that you were involved in things that you weren't.** They may be able to figure it out and you would be disqualified, but even more importantly, if you did get the scholarship you would have cheated someone else out of it, who deserved it.

6) **Do <u>exactly</u> what they ask of you.** If they want a one page essay, don't give them a one and a half page essay. If they want it in by a certain date, make sure it gets there in time. If they request a recommendation, give them one. Sometimes all it takes is one missing requirement to disqualify a person for a scholarship, so make sure you don't forget *anything*.

7) **Don't force anything.** If it asks for an essay "no longer than" two pages, don't feel like you have to *fill up* a full two pages. If your essay is only one and a half pages and you feel like you don't have any more to say, don't force yourself to complete the two pages. If you do, you'll just wind up with some garbage that might be detrimental to your essay.

Additional Resources

Financial Aid Books

Complete College Financing Guide, 2nd edition
Barron's Educational Services
$13.95

College Costs & Financial Aid Handbook:
The College Board
$16.00

How to Pay for College
By: Richard B. Lyttle and Frank Farrara

Free Money for College, 3rd edition
By: Laurie Blum
$24.95

Free Money for College from the Government
By: Laurie Blum
$14.95

Free Money from Colleges and Universities
By: Laurie Blum
$14.95

The Complete Scholarship Book
Student Services, Inc.
$22.95

The A's and B's of Academic Scholarships
Ann Schimke - Editor
$7.50

How to Maintain Maximum College Financial Aid
By: Edward H. Rosenwasse
How to Get to College for Free
By: Linda Bowman
$9.95

America's Lowest Cost Colleges
By: Nicholas A. Roes
$9.95

Looking Beyond the Ivy League
By: Loren Pope
$7.95

Other Books

Writing a Successful College Application Essay
(Barron's) By: George Ehrenhaft

The Next Step: College
By: Gail Andrews Bates
$11.95

Study Guides

Cracking the A.C.T.
Princeton Review
$17.00

Cracking the S.A.T. and P.S.A.T.
Princeton Review
$17.00

Test Taking Strategies
By: Judi Kesselman-Turkel and Franklynn Peterson
$2.45

Up Your Grades
By: Ann Hunt Tufariello
$12.95

Websites

http://www.studentservices.com/fastweb

http://www.finaid.org

Phone Numbers

1-800-433-3243   Federal Student Aid Information Center

Chapter Thirteen
Reaching Your Goals

In Chapter One you set your goals. Now you are ready to achieve them. The key to reaching any goal is to develop a plan. Think about what steps you will have to take to make them happen. Some of your goals will require a plan completely free of financial matters. For example, if one person's goal is to make the varsity soccer team, the only way to attain that goal would be through hard work and practice. You could enhance your plan by adding specific times to practice and designing work-out patterns to follow, but the basic principle of your plan would be, "Work for it." If it is a financial goal you must create a plan for, the principle remains the same, "Work for it."

There are a few different plans and systems you can use to reach your goals depending on what type of goal it is and what kind of person you are. If it is a short-term financial goal, such as Gail's goal to go to the spring dance, and you are a person who can handle limitations, use the following the steps to aid you in creating a plan.

How to Create Your Own Plan to Achieve a Short-Term Financial Goal

Note: This type of goal plan will first evaluate your income, fixed expenses, and cost of reaching your goal, and then show you how to set a limit on your spending in the meantime so that you can reach it. You can use the blank chart to fill in the information for each step and you can use Gail's short-term goal as a guide.

1) Determine the **number of weeks you have until the goal must be met**.

2) Determine approximately how much money you will make until the time that you want your goal accomplished. This is called your "**Means of Payment.**"

3) Determine the **total of all the fixed expenses** that you will encounter throughout that time period. (Fixed expenses are things that you *must* pay for, no matter what. Ex. $65 for car insurance each month)

4) Subtract your fixed expenses from your total income (Step #2 minus Step #3), to find how much **money you will have to work with**.

5) Determine the **cost of meeting your goal**. If it is flexible, knowing how much money you will have to work with will help you determine how much you are willing to spend.

If the price of meeting your goal is less than the money you have to work with (amount from Step #4), congratulations, you can do it, but you still have a little more planning to do. If not, you may need to make some adjustments. Try to find a way to make more money or to reduce the cost of your goal.

Now you know how much your goal will cost and you know how much money you will have to work with to get it, but what money will you be living on in the meantime? To be certain that you don't spend the money that you planned on having, you're going to have to determine what your spending limit will be for other expenses (that are not fixed and were not included in Step #3). Use the following steps in order to determine what that limit will be.

6) Subtract the cost of the goal from the amount you have to work with. (Step #4 minus Step #5.) This is how much **extra money you can afford to spend** until your goal must be accomplished.

7) Divide the amount from Step #7 by the number of weeks you have until the goal must be met (from Step #1). This is **your weekly limit**. You cannot spend more than this amount per week, on your variable expenses, if your goal is to be accomplished. Your weekly limit is how much you can spend per week, on top of the fixed expenses you already considered in Step #3. If it's time to pay your car insurance, you're entitled to the $65 for the car insurance plus *your* money for the week.

Good Luck!!!

Short-Term Goal

_____
(Write *your* short-term goal here.)

1) Date goal must be reached by: _____
   Number of weeks away: _____

2) **Means of Payment**   **Amount**
   a) _____   _____
   b) _____   _____
   c) _____   _____
                          Total: _____

3) **Fixed Expenses**
   a) _____   _____
   b) _____   _____
   c) _____   _____
   d) _____   _____
   e) _____   _____
                          Total: _____

4) **Means of Payment**   _____
   - Fixed Expenses   _____
   = Total Money Available   _____

5) **Cost of Goal** (There are different blanks to add up various counterpart costs of reaching your goal.)
   a) _____   _____
   b) _____   _____
   c) _____   _____
   d) _____   _____
   e) _____   _____
                          Total: _____

6) **Total Money Available**   _____
   - Cost of Goal   _____
   = Money for Variable Expenses _____

7) **Money for Variable Expenses**   _____
   Divided by Number of Weeks   ÷ _____
   = Weekly Spending Limit   _____

On the previous page is an example of a financial plan for meeting a short-term goal. This would be a perfect plan for Gail to use to determine how she could reach her goal of going to the spring dance, called "Sponge." In order to do this, she had to first figure out how much money she would have to work with and then determine what her spending limit would have to be so that she would have enough money to go to the dance.

To determine her means of payment, Gail thought about how many paychecks she would receive and what other money she would make before the dance. The dance was nine weeks away so she could expect nine paychecks, each worth about $65. So the total amount she expected to earn from work by the time of the dance was $585. She also watched her aunt and uncle's house and dog while they were on vacation, so she was expecting about $160 from them (they were very generous). So it was estimated that she would make about $745 by the time of the "Sponge" dance. You might look at this number and think, "Of course Gail will have enough money to go to the dance," but you can't be too sure about that yet. You also have to consider what her expenses are going to be up until the time of the dance.

At the time, Gail owed her mom $86.70, so that was the first thing she would have to pay for. Then, she would have to pay for car insurance for both the months of January and February ($65 a piece). She also would have to spend about $75 in gas between then and the dance. Her dad's birthday was coming up and so was Valentine's Day. Gifts for each of those would be about $30. She also planned on giving about $30 for her church offering by the time of the dance. All of the fixed expenses totaled $381.70. Finally, she subtracted her fixed expenses from the total means of payment. This amount, $363.30, is the total amount of money she would have leftover for the dance and variable expenses in the meantime.

Now Gail had to figure out how much the dance would cost. Knowing that she wouldn't have much to work with, and considering she would also have to use part of this money for food and leisure for the next nine weeks, she tried to scrimp and save wherever she could. For example, you'll notice that on her goal plan there is no expense listed for a new dress. That's because she decided she would listen to her mother and borrow one of her sister's, but she still needed to get a new pair of shoes (her sister's were a little big). Also notice that it's only going to cost her $12 to get her hair done. Unrealistic? No, she gets her hair done at a beauty school for $10 (plus a $2 tip). She found that they do a better job there than at the more expensive beauty salons. You have to remember that the people at the beauty school are being *graded* on your hair, and there are always instructors there to help or take over if you're unsatisfied. For dinner she only planned on spending $60. If she had more money she might have chosen a fancier place, but the restaurant she did decide on has excellent food and reasonable prices. Tickets would be about $25, pictures about $15 (for the cheapest package), and the little pin-on flower, about $5. So, what is the $100 in "Other" for? Well, Gail didn't want to wind up short of cash on a fancy date, so she wanted to have some extra money just in case. Then, she wasn't sure what plans might emerge after the dance, so she wanted some extra money for that, too. The total cost of the dance was estimated to be $247.

To determine what her spending limit would be so that she would have enough money, she subtracted the cost of the goal from her "Total Money Available." ($363.30 - $247.00 = $116.30) According to this she could spend a maximum of $116.30 on variable expenses in the next nine weeks, which averages out to about $13.00 a week. It would be to Gail's advantage not to spend exactly $13 a week, but spend less whenever possible. This is always a good idea in case you forgot to factor something in while making your goal plan or an unexpected expense comes up. You should also note that even if you have a savings account, with all the money you need in it, it's still a good idea to plan for short-term goals like this, instead of simply depleting your savings.

Gail's Short-Term Goal to Go to the Spring Dance

1) Date goal must be reached by: <u>3/16/01</u>
         Number of weeks away: <u>9 weeks</u>

2) Means of Payment
      a)   House-sitting $160
      b)   Work (9 checks x $65) $585
                                      Total: $745

3) Fixed Expenses
      a)   Current Debt $86.70
      b)   January car insurance $65
      c)   Dad's Birthday $30
      d)   Valentine's Day $30
      e)   February car insurance $65
      f)   Gas $75
      g)   Church Offering $30
      h)   Living Expenses ($10 a week) $100
                                      Total: $381.70

4) Means of Payment
      $745
      - Fixed Expenses   **$381.70**
      = Total Money Available   **$363.30**

5) Expenses
      a)   Shoes $30
      b)   Hair $12
      c)   Dinner $60
      d)   Tickets $25
      e)   Pictures $15
      f)   Boutonniere $ 5
      g)   Other $100
                                      Total: $247

6) Total Money Available   **$363.30**
      - Cost of Goal   **- $247.00**
      = Money for Variable Expenses   **$116.30**

7) Money for Variable Expenses Divided by 9   **$12.92**

There are some other ways you can plan for a goal. One way is quite the opposite from the one you just learned. The first financial plan for a short-term goal is a good one to start with. It puts you on a spending budget so that you can plan in advance to meet your goal. It's also good for goals with rigid deadlines. The other type of financial plan allows you to set a savings goal, in order to attain your actual goal, as opposed to setting a spending limit. This type of plan can be useful for any type of goal, especially ones with flexible deadlines. This is how it works:

Let's say you wanted to save up $3000 to buy a used car. Your parents said that if you save up half of the money, they would loan you the other half. That way you can have use of the car while you're still paying for it, and since your parents are nice, they won't charge you interest. You're one year away from getting your license. To save the $1500 by the time you get your license, you must save about $30 a week ($1500 divided by 52, since there are 52 weeks in a year). If you can get a job that pays about $70 a week, this could be quite feasible. Every week that you get paid, put $30 in the bank automatically. If you have more to spare, or if you came a little short last week, put in more. Stick to your plan and you'll have saved enough money to reach your goal.

This is one of the simplest ways to plan for a financial goal. Set a date for your goal and set the amount you must save for it weekly. If, however, it seems that the amount you must save weekly is a little unlikely, you may need to allow yourself more time to reach your goal or try to earn more money. Once you figure it out, stick to it, and soon your goal will become a reality.

TIPS for Goal Setting and Goal Getting

1) **Don't rule anything out!** Don't limit yourself to what you *know* you can do. If you're not sure if you can do it, try it anyway.

2) **Be confident** in yourself and your abilities.

3) **If you really want to do something, do it!** Don't let any foolish reasons hold you back.

4) **Be reasonable.** Don't plan on saving $50 a week to reach your goal if you only make $55. This obviously wouldn't work, so there is no point in pretending.

5) **Create a plan that will work.** If you know what you want to do, you also need to know *how* you're going to do it.

6) **Stick to your plan.** Your plan is worthless if you don't follow it.

7) **Focus yourself.** You know what you want and you have a plan. Center yourself on reaching it, and nothing can stop you. (This is why it's a good idea to keep a poster of your main goal in your room, as suggested in Chapter One. This will keep you focused on reaching it.)

Additional Resources

<u>Books</u>

Wishcraft: How to Get Everything What You Really Want
By: Barbara Sher
$12.00

Glossary

Annual Percentage Rate   -the percentage return per year expected on an investment or the annual percentage of a loan that must be paid for interest

Assets   -items that are a source of value; For example, cash, a bank account balance, a car, a house, etc. are all assets.

Budget   -a financial plan developed to reach a specific savings goal or to remain within a designated spending limit

Capital Gains   -earnings above the cost of an investment; For example, when a stock price rises above the amount that the person paid for it, that person has a capital gain.

Certificate of Deposit   -a savings tool in which the saver loans the bank a designated amount of money for a set period of time at a particular interest rate

Compounding   -when interest is earned on both the principal of the investment as well as the previously earned interest; Example: If you invest $1000 and make 10% the first year, you will make $100 in interest and have $1100. The next year you will make $110, due to the power of compounding, and will have $1210.

Credit   -the amount which a person, corporation, or business may be financially trusted with in a given case

Credit Standing   -reputation for meeting financial obligations, paying bills, etc.; the perceived willingness and ability of an individual or business to pay back borrowed funds

Dependent   -a person who is financially supported by someone else; Example: A teenager is a dependent of his or her parents, since the parents typically cover the majority of the teenager's living expenses, such as food, shelter, and clothing.

Diversification   -an investment strategy in which investments are divided between a variety of different assets; For example, a person may diversify their investments by saving 30% in bonds, 20% in cash, and 50% in stocks. They can diversify further by investing in different types of stocks and bonds. For example, a person may invest in some growth stocks and some income stocks or some short-term bonds and some long-term bonds.

Dividends	-earnings that are paid out to investors; Example: Companies pay out a portion of their profits to their stockholders in the form of dividends.
Expenditures	-money spent for basic necessities, leisure activities, personal items, and several other items; the amount of income that is spent
FDIC	-Federal Deposit Insurance Corporation, insures bank account deposits up to $100,000
Goal	-an objective that an individual consciously strives to achieve
Income	-funds that a person receives through paid employment, returns on investment, gifts, or other means
Interest	-the amount of money that is paid by one individual (or entity) to another for the use of their funds; the price paid by the borrower to borrow money and the income received by the lender for lending the money; Examples: You receive interest on your bank account because you are lending the bank your money. If you take out a loan to buy a car, you must pay interest to borrow the funds.
Liability	-money or assets owed; A mortgage on a home or a loan on a car are liabilities.
Maturity	-when an investment reaches its designated lifespan; For example, a U.S. Savings Bond will reach maturity when its actual value is equivalent to its face value. (If you bought a $50 bond for $25, the bond would be mature when it is worth $50.) Some investments have set maturities, such as one, five, ten, or thirty years.
Mutual Fund	-a pool of money that is invested by a professional manager; Each investor buys shares in the fund and is compensated for earned returns by an increase in the share price or paid dividends.
NCUA	-National Credit Union Administration, insures credit union accounts up to $100,000
Net Worth	-assets minus liabilities; Your net worth represents what you would have left if you were to cash in all of your assets and pay all of your bills.

Prospectus	-an informative booklet that explains the potential risks and rewards from a given investment
Stock	-ownership in a company; When a person owns stock in a company, they essentially own a piece of the company and thus are entitled to a proportionate share of that company's profits.
U.S. Savings Bonds	-a savings tool in which the saver lends the government money; The saver purchases a bond, which is essentially an I.O.U. from the government. The saver can then redeem their money at some point in the future by taking the bond to the bank and cashing it in.
W-2	-a document sent out at the beginning of the year summarizing wages and taxes paid for the previous year, utilized to complete tax forms; Only individuals who have earned taxable income over the prior year will receive a W-2

Websites

- http://www.aaii.com – American Association of Individual Investors

- http://www.americasaves.org – America Saves

- http://www.better-investing.org – Better Investing

- http://www.businessweek.com – Business Week

- http://www.careers.com – Explore Different Careers

- http://www.collegeboard.com – Thinking about Tomorrow

- http://www.collegesavings.org – College Savings

- http://www.consumerworld.com – Consumer World

- http://www.cnnfn.com – CNN

- http://www.creditinfocenter.com – Credit Info Center

- http://www.equifax.com – Equifax Credit Information Services

- http://www.experian.com – Experian (credit bureau)

- http://www.fastweb.com – Student Financing Information

- http://www.fidelity.com – Fidelity Investments

- http://www.finaid.org – Smart Student Guide to Financial Aid

- http://www.financewise.com – Finance Search Engine

- http://www.financial-education.org – Financial Education

- http://www.financiallearning.com – Financial Learning

- http://www.fool.com – The Motley Fool

- http://www.highschoolstartups.com – High School Startups

- http://www.homefair.com/homefair/cmr/salcalc.html – The Salary Calculator

- http://www.ici.org – The Investment Company Institute

- http://www.infoplease.com/ipa/A0855786.html – Cost of Living Index for Selected Cities

- http://www.investoreducation.org – Investor Education

- http://www.irs.gov – Internal Revenue Service Website

- http://www.italladdsup.org – It All Adds Up

- http://www.jobweb.com/Resumes_Interviews/resume_guide/restips.html – Job Web Resume Guide

- http://www.KristiRichards.com – Personal Finance Resources and Information

- http://www.kiplinger.com – Kiplinger's

- http://www.money.com – Money

- http://www.moneycentral.com – Money Central

- http://www.myfuture.com – My Future

- http://www.myvesta.org – Financial Help for Everyone

- http://www.nfcc.org – National Foundation for Credit Counseling

- http://ourworld.compuserve.com/homepages/Bonehead_Finance – Bonehead Finance

- http://www.wa.gov/ago/teenconsumer – Consumer Education for Teens

- http://www.savingsbonds.gov – Savings Bonds

- http://www.sec.gov/investor/students.shtml – Resources for Students

- http://www.smartmoney.com – Smart Money

- http://www.stretcher.com – The Dollar Stretcher

- http://www.teenstartups.com – Teen Startups

- http://www.transunion.com – Trans Union Corporation

- http://www.vanguard.com – Vanguard

- http://www.wsrn.com – Wall Street Research Net

- http://www.wiredscholar.com – Understand The Costs of College

- http://wsjclassroomedition.com – Wall Street Journal Classroom Edition

- http://www.youngbiz.com – Young Biz

- http://www.youngentrepreneur.com – Young Entrepreneur

- http://www.youngmoney.com – Young Money

- http://loan.yahoo.com/c – Yahoo Credit Information

- http://www.yourcredit.com – Your Credit

Date	Car	Personal	Clothing	Leisure	Food	Gifts	Other	Income
Budgeted								
Totals								
Difference								
Ttl.Income								
Ttl. Spent								
Ttl. Saved								

Date	Car	Personal	Clothing	Leisure	Food	Gifts	Other	Income
Budgeted								
Totals								
Difference								
Ttl.Income								
Ttl. Spent								
Ttl. Saved								

Date	Car	Personal	Clothing	Leisure	Food	Gifts	Other	Income
Budgeted								
Totals								
Difference								
Ttl.Income								
Ttl. Spent								
Ttl. Saved								

	Credit Card	Credit Card Number	Credit Limit	Expira-tion	Phone Number
1					
2					
3					
4					
5					
6					
7					

Date	Place of Purchase	Amount	Balance	Amt. To be Paid on*:	

Date	Place of Purchase	Amount	Balance	Amt. To be Paid on*:

Date	Place of Purchase	Amount	Balance	Amt. To be Paid on*:	

Scholarship Applications

Scholarship:_____

Due:_____

Include:_____

_____

_____

Notified by:_____

Mailed:_____

Scholarship:_____

Due:_____

Include:_____

_____

_____

Notified by:_____

Mailed:_____

Scholarship:_____

Due:_____

Include:_____

_____

_____

Notified by:_____

Mailed:_____

Scholarship:_____

Due:_____

Include:_____

_____

_____

Notified by:_____

Mailed:_____

Scholarship Applications

Scholarship:_____

Due:_____

Include:_____

_____

_____

Notified by:_____

Mailed:_____

Scholarship:_____

Due:_____

Include:_____

_____

_____

Notified by:_____

Mailed:_____

Scholarship:_____

Due:_____

Include:_____

_____

_____

Notified by:_____

Mailed:_____

Scholarship:_____

Due:_____

Include:_____

_____

_____

Notified by:_____

Mailed:_____

Scholarship Applications

Scholarship:_____

Due:_____

Include:_____

_____

_____

Notified by:_____

Mailed:_____

Scholarship:_____

Due:_____

Include:_____

_____

_____

Notified by:_____

Mailed:_____

Scholarship:_____

Due:_____

Include:_____

_____

_____

Notified by:_____

Mailed:_____

Scholarship:_____

Due:_____

Include:_____

_____

_____

Notified by:_____

Mailed:_____

Visit

http://www.KristiRichards.com

For More Information On...

- Personal Finance and Investing

- How to start your own Finance Club

- How to have Kristi Richards guest speak for your school, class, club, or organization

Also...

- Email the author

- Read and submit questions

- Access worksheets and discover valuable resources

- Join an online group and participate in live chats

To Order Additional Books, Please Visit:
http://www.KristiRichards.com